THE MAGNET, THE METHOD AND THE MACHINE

The 3 Laws and 9 Levers Custom Homebuilders
Use to Scale to $20M and Beyond

RODRIC LENHART

ISBN 979-8-9881359-2-0

Million Dollar Flip Flops Media
Charlotte NC

TABLE OF CONTENTS

Introduction 1

Owner vs. Operator: The Mindset That Changes Everything........7

Law 1: The Magnet 21
    Lever 1: Niche & Differentiation 23
    Lever 2: Lead Flow Engine 33
    Lever 3: Premium Client Conversion 45

Law 2: The Machine 59
    Lever 4: Structured for Scale 63
    Lever 5: Team Leadership 77
    Lever 6: Culture by Design... 89

Law 3: The Method... 103
    Lever 7: World-Class Client Experience 105
    Lever 8: Predictable Job Flow: Scaling chaos → broke faster. . 117
    Lever 9: Profit & Time Mastery 131

From Builder to CEO.. 141

About the Author.. 153

INTRODUCTION

"The best time to plant a tree was 20 years ago. The second best time is now." — Ancient Proverb

Why This Book Is Different

When I first sat down to write this book, the manuscript ballooned to more than 50,000 words. That's the curse of someone who has spent decades in the trenches: I wanted to give you *everything*.

> ⌐▶ **Real Talk:** I don't believe in wasting your time. Builders like you don't need another padded business book filled with buzzwords and endless theory. You also don't need my life story in every chapter (you can read *Million Dollar Flip Flops* for that). You need clarity. You need direction. You need tools you can put to work immediately.

So I cut it in half. Every page you're about to read has been distilled down to what actually matters. No filler. No generic advice. Just the proven frameworks—the 3 Laws and 9 Levers—that will get you out of the expensive prison you've built for yourself and into the role of a true CEO.

This isn't the book you read once and shelve. It's the one you keep open on your desk, dog-ear, and revisit as you implement.

What You'll Discover Inside

In the pages ahead, you'll find the exact framework I've used to help builders push past their ceiling...whether that's $4M or $40M—without losing their sanity or sacrificing standards. You'll discover how to:

- Turn a pile of chaotic projects into a streamlined, scalable operation
- Step out of being the bottleneck and build a team that makes smart decisions without you
- Apply the 9 Levers that boost profitability while cutting your personal workload
- Position your company as the premium choice in your market—attracting clients who value quality, not discounts
- Reclaim time freedom without lowering the bar that built your reputation
- Build true wealth - both in time and money - that will allow you to make an impact

None of this is theory. Every strategy comes straight from the trenches of not only my own companies spanning 30+ years of experience in real estate, development, and construction, but also real custom homebuilding businesses coast to coast, facing the same battles you are. These strategies work—if you work them.

A Word of Thanks

This book is possible because of the builders who trusted me, allowed me into their businesses, and let me learn from both their wins and their struggles. Every principle here has been forged in their experiences alongside my own.

I want to thank my partner, my ride-or-die, Nichole. You were with me when I had nothing, when the only thing I could offer was a dream and the grit to chase it. You believed in me before the success, before the books, before the coaching, before seeing the world. You said you'd stand by me even if it meant living under a bridge, and I've never forgotten. You stood tall when everything felt uncertain. I would go to war with you. I would die for you. If the world were a hurricane, being with you is like standing in the eye, calm and steady while the storm rages around us.

The sacrifices I make now — writing this book, pouring into others at the highest level, and yes, even wrestling with my classic car obsession that takes up the garage and way too much time — are all for us. For the life we've built, and the one we're still building. There is no one else I would want by my side. With you, the impossible isn't just a dream — it's our reality.

And to the team at *Send a Student Leader Abroad* - our nonprofit - to which 100% of the proceeds of both books are donated. Thank you for proving that the principles of business transformation ripple far beyond the bottom line. Watching you empower entrepreneurial students with life-changing international experiences reminds me to think bigger about the impact of this work.

Your Next New Foundation

By picking up this book, you've already taken the first step toward building something new. You're ready to pour a stronger foundation—one that supports not just a bigger company, but a better life.

Thoreau said, *"The cost of anything is the amount of life you exchange for it."* My hope is that what follows helps you create a business that demands less of your life while delivering more of what truly matters: freedom, impact, and the satisfaction of building something exceptional.

Turn the page. Let's begin the work of creating a company that stands the test of time—a business that works for you, not the other way around.

The escape plan starts now.

Your Hidden Bonus Awaits

Every chapter in this book unlocks a deeper level of tools, trainings, and step-by-step guides I normally reserve for private clients. Think of it as the *hidden door* — videos, templates, and frameworks you can put to work today to implement what you're learning.

Scan the QR code if you don't like typing or visit www.builderstimemachine.com/bonus to access it now.

OWNER VS. OPERATOR: THE MINDSET THAT CHANGES EVERYTHING

I'll save you some time right now. If you take nothing else from this book, take this: the single biggest shift you must make is moving from operator to owner.

Because if you don't make this mindset transition, nothing else I've outlined here will stick. You can install all the dashboards, implement all the processes, and polish all the client experiences in the world, but if you're still thinking like an operator, you'll keep defaulting back to firefighting mode.

The Trap of the Operator

An **operator** is self-employed. They've got freedom in theory, but in reality, they're exhausted. They *are* the business. Every problem flows through them. Every decision requires their sign-off.

When someone tells me, "I'm just so burnt out," I already know what's happening. They're an operator, not an owner.

And it's not just semantics. Its identity.

Operators start because they're good at something. A top salesperson thinks, *"Why am I closing all these deals for someone else? I'll just start my own thing."* A project manager decides, *"I'm basically running these jobs already—might as well do it for myself."*

In the beginning, it works. Someone says, "I want a green house." You go build a green house. Simple enough. But soon the calls pile up, the projects overlap, and suddenly you're no longer building—you're scrambling.

Herb's Burgers vs. McDonald's

Picture the little burger shack in your hometown. Maybe it was called Herb's. Line out the door. Best burger in town. And 30 years later, Herb is still behind the counter, flipping patties.

Now, let me ask you—does McDonald's have the best burger? No. But they sell more burgers than anyone on the planet and 100X more than poor old Herb. Why? Because someone figured out how to **scale**.

Herb stayed an operator. Ray Kroc became an owner.

And that's the choice staring you in the face.

The Psychology of Ownership

80% of success is psychology. Only 20% is strategy. Most builders already *know* things they should be doing differently. It's not a lack of knowledge—it's a lack of mindset.

Operators live in fear. They say:

- "I can't hire anyone else because I can't afford them."
- "Nobody will do it as well as me."
- "If I don't control every detail, it'll all fall apart."

Owners push through that fear. They recognize it, feel it, and move anyway.

└┈▶ **Real Talk:** When times are uncertain, most people freeze. They hold back. They shrink. But shrinking is a self-fulfilling prophecy. The businesses that thrive in uncertain times are led by owners who see beyond the moment. They understand—it's not the economy, it's not your town, it's not your labor pool - it's your psychology.

When you're going through hell? Keep going. That's the owner's mindset.

The Hidden Cost of Operating

Operators don't just slow growth—they sabotage it.

Every new hire feels like babysitting. Every new project feels like another weight on your back. You spend more time putting out fires than building a future. You become the world's most expensive employee in your own company.

I've watched countless builders fall into this trap. Their revenue grows, but their life shrinks. They thought they were building a business. In reality, they just built themselves a more elaborate cage.

The Owner's Advantage

Owners, on the other hand, know their real job: solving problems and building systems.

They understand problems aren't proof something's broken—they're proof you're in business. Proof you're human. Proof you're alive. Problems are raw material. They sculpt your company, your leadership, and yes—your soul.

Owners don't run from problems. They don't waste energy blaming the economy, their team, or the market. They face problems, solve them, and move on.

And here's the paradox: when you stop being the operator and step into ownership, you don't become less valuable—you become more valuable. You stop being the bottleneck and start being the architect.

That's when scaling becomes possible. That's when your company stops being an expensive prison and starts being a true asset.

The Gatekeeper

So let me be blunt: if you're still thinking like an operator, you can skip the rest of this book. You'll just collect more "ideas" that never get implemented.

But if you're ready to make the psychological shift from operator to owner—if you're ready to step into the role of leader, problem-solver, and architect of your business—then every lever and every law I've laid out here will transform your business and your life.

The choice is yours: do you want to flip burgers forever, or do you want to build an empire?

Perfect. I'm glad you're still here.

Let's get started.

The "Structural Ceiling"

Every builder hits it.

That invisible wall where growth no longer feels like momentum — it feels like quicksand.

At first, the ceiling is subtle. You're busy, jobs are moving, referrals keep coming, and the calendar looks full. But instead of feeling a sense of progress, you feel… stuck.

This is the **Structural Ceiling**. And it has nothing to do with how hard you work or the number of hours you put in. It's not about better spreadsheets, shinier project management software, or another flavor-of-the-month leadership book.

The pain of scaling comes down to one thing: **structure.**

Most builders I meet are running their companies the same way they ran their first million-dollar year. Same communication patterns. Same seat-of-the-pants scheduling. Same "just figure it out" mentality. That works — until it doesn't.

> ⌐▶ **Real Talk:** The business you're running right now is perfectly designed to give you the results you're currently getting. If you're at $4M, $8M, maybe even $12M, and you're stuck in the mud — that's not a fluke. That's the *design*.

And design is what creates the **Structural Ceiling**.

It's why the jump from $5M to $10M or $10M to $20M feels like running uphill with a piano strapped to your back.

It's why "just one more hire" doesn't solve the chaos.

It's why no matter how many hours you put in, the company never truly runs without you.

Scaling pain is not a spreadsheet problem. It's a structural problem.

And until you learn to build a new structure — one that actually supports growth — you'll keep smacking your head against the same ceiling, wondering why it hurts so much.

The "Expensive Prison"

Most builders I meet don't own their own businesses. They own a very expensive prison.

Here's what I mean:

- Their phone buzzes 24/7.
- Every decision runs through them.
- Clients, subs, employees — everyone is texting the "warden" for permission before they move an inch.

And the crazy part? *They built this prison themselves.*

Every time they said, "It's faster if I just do it."

Every time they avoided setting up systems because the job "had to get done right now."

Every time they kept control instead of building structure.

Brick by brick, text by text, they locked themselves inside.

And the harder they work, the tighter the chains get.

It doesn't matter if you're doing $3M or $30M — if the business relies on you to make every decision, you're not free. You're just a higher-paid, higher-stressed employee of your own company.

That's the **Expensive Prison**: plenty of revenue, zero freedom.

My Story

I didn't learn this in a textbook. I learned it the hard way.

I grew up in a small town in Michigan in a tiny 1-bath house on a very busy road. No silver spoon, no shortcuts. I went to bed most nights listening to my parents argue about money. I didn't know where I was headed yet, I just knew I wanted freedom — to build something that gave me choices.

By my twenties, I had started and sold multiple companies. Eventually, I had real estate, development, construction, and property management companies and several hundred million dollars in sales under my belt.

From the outside, it looked like success. Inside, I was drowning.

Every decision, every fire, every late-night email landed on my desk. My calendar was full, my phone never stopped, and everyone around me thought I was "winning."

But the truth?

I was stuck in the same **Expensive Prison** you're probably living in right now.

That's when I realized something: **hard work wasn't the answer.**

Structure was.

Once I built the right framework — the 3 Laws and 9 Levers you're about to learn — everything changed. My business ran without me. I got my time back. I exited for more than I ever imagined.

And that's why I'm writing this book. Because I've been where you are, and I know what it feels like to wonder if the pain will ever stop.

The good news is, it can. You just need a different plan and someone who has been in your shoes to light the way forward.

The Stakes

Let's be clear: if you don't change the way you're building your business...well... nothing changes.

It's the "owner" who will live the same year 75 times in a row, call it a life, and die.

Blunt? Yes. Reality? Also yes.

The problems don't magically disappear with more revenue. They compound.

- At $5M, it's late nights and missed family dinners.
- At $10M, it's broken systems, angry clients, bad reviews and good employees walking out the door.
- At $20M, it's burnout so deep you're ready to sell just to breathe again...and one bad move can cost you everything. Literally.

I've watched too many builders scale themselves straight into misery. They think the next hire, the next piece of software, or the next project will be the fix.

It never is.

> ⌐▶ **Real Talk:** The thing that got you here — your grit, your hustle, your ability to muscle through — is the exact thing holding you back from going further.

Ignore the 3 Laws, and the ceiling doesn't just stay in place — it lowers. The more you push, the harder it pushes back.

That's the cost of staying the same: **a bigger business with the same problems... multiplied.**

Imagine This

Your business runs without you. You're not just taking weekends off; you've reduced your working hours by a significant 30% while maintaining or even increasing your net profit margin. Projects flow predictably, removing the constant guesswork and anxiety that may have plagued you in the past. Clients are thrilled—and they're the right clients, not the wrong ones (we'll discuss this in depth later).

Your team knows exactly what to do, when to do it, and how to win without you hovering over them.

You take a week off... and nothing breaks.

You step out of the field... and profit doesn't disappear.

You sit at the dinner table with your family, fully present, because your phone isn't buzzing like a slot machine in Vegas.

> **⌐····▶ Real Talk:** When this doesn't happen, I call it "giving your wife and kids the finger"... not that one... the one that implies, "This client is more important than you right now." You might not say it, but they feel it.

Remember, this isn't about information. It's about transformation.

It's also not a fantasy. It's what happens when you stop trying to *work harder* and start building differently.

By the end of this book, you'll know exactly how to escape the prison, break through the ceiling, and finally become what your company, and your family, has needed all along: a **strategic CEO, not an overwhelmed operator.**

The 3 Laws and 9 Levers – Your Escape Plan

Before we take this ride together, let me show you the roadmap.

Every builder who breaks through the ceiling and scales with freedom masters three unbreakable laws. Within each law are three levers, nine in total. Pull the right lever at the right time, and you create momentum. Ignore them, and you stay stuck. Here they are:

Law 1: The Magnet (Marketing & Positioning)

- **Lever 1 – Niche & Differentiation:** Stop being everything to everyone and plant your flag where you win.

- **Lever 2 – Lead Flow Engine:** Build a predictable pipeline so you're not at the mercy of referrals.

- **Lever 3 – Premium Client Conversion:** Filter out the tire-kickers and close the right clients at the right price.

Law 2: The Machine (Team & Structure)

- **Lever 4 – Right People in the Right Seats:** Put the right talent in the right roles, so the business runs without you.

- **Lever 5 – Structured for Scale:** Build an organizational foundation that grows with you, not against you.

- **Lever 6 – Performance Feedback Loops:** Create rhythms and scorecards that keep your team aligned and accountable.

Law 3: The Method (Systems & Execution)

- **Lever 7 – World-Class Client Experience:** Turn jobs into a repeatable process that delights clients and builds reputation.

- **Lever 8 – Predictable Job Flow:** Systematize scheduling, estimating, and project flow so profit is consistent.

- **Lever 9 – Profit & Time Mastery:** Maximize both dollars and hours by aligning tech, systems, and time with your highest leverage.

The 3 Laws and 9 Levers are not a theory. They're the blueprint I've used to help builders like you scale past the ceiling — some to $20M, $30M, and $40M, and others to exits they never thought possible (including myself).

Bottom line: all of them used it to finally break free from the Structural Ceiling and the Expensive Prison.

Now that you know the map, we'll start where the journey always begins — **The Magnet.**

PS — Don't make the mistake of jumping straight to the lever you *think* is your problem. If even one of the nine isn't functioning, the whole framework eventually collapses. It fails quietly at first, then all at once. Trust the process. Remember: work the system—because the system works.

Your Hidden Bonus Awaits

Every chapter in this book unlocks a deeper level of tools, trainings, and step-by-step guides I normally reserve for private clients. Think of it as the *hidden door* — videos, templates, and frameworks you can put to work today to implement what you're learning.

Scan the QR code if you don't like typing or visit www.builderstimemachine.com/bonus to access it now.

LAW 1

THE MAGNET

The Million Dollar Flip Flops Story

When I first started in business, I had one strategy: say yes to everything.

Every client, every job, every opportunity. If someone had money and wanted me to build, I was in. That's how I ended up exhausted, juggling projects I didn't care about, for clients who drained the life out of me.

At the time, I thought saying yes meant I was growing. In reality, I was digging a hole.

That season of my life led to my best-selling book, *Million Dollar Flip Flops*. It's not a story about building the perfect company. It's about burning myself out chasing other people's definitions of success — and realizing the cost of trying to be all things to all people... and it nearly cost me everything...literally.

> ⌐⋯➤ **Real Talk:** When you're everything to everyone, you're valuable to no one.

The builders I coach have fallen into the same trap. They chase every lead, bid every job, and convince themselves that more work is always better. But instead of momentum, what they really build is exhaustion.

The lesson I had to learn — and the lesson you'll learn in this chapter — is that growth doesn't come from doing more. It comes from doing the right things, for the right clients, in the right way.

And it starts with carving out a **niche** and standing out through **differentiation.**

LEVER 1

NICHE & DIFFERENTIATION

"The man who chases two rabbits catches neither."
– Confucius

Positioning is Foundational

Every builder wants more leads, better clients, and bigger jobs.

> ∟▶ **Real Talk:** None of that matters if the market doesn't know exactly who you are, what you stand for, and why you're different. That's positioning—and it's the foundation of everything else.

Positioning isn't just marketing. It's identity. It's the story people tell about your business when you're not in the room. Get it right, and you become the obvious choice. Get it wrong, and you're just another name in the bid pile.

The first step is clarity:

- Who exactly is your ideal client?

- What problems do you solve better than anyone else?
- What jobs should you stop saying "yes" to, so you can dominate the ones that matter?

Most builders define their market too broadly—"homeowners," "commercial clients," "anyone who can pay." That's not positioning, that's desperation. The power comes from focus. Saying no to what doesn't fit creates the space to excel where you do.

The 3 Levers of Positioning

1. Market Differentiation – Define and communicate your unique value. What do you do better, faster, or smarter than anyone else?

2. Client Selection – Choose who you work with, and set criteria so you attract the right clients while respectfully directing others elsewhere.

3. Service Offering – Decide what you will—and won't— provide. Package it, price it, and structure it so it delivers maximum value for the client and profit for you.

Positioning is the magnet. It determines who's drawn to you, how they perceive your value, and whether you're seen as a commodity or the clear market leader.

Lighthouse vs. Flashlight

Most builders run their businesses like a flashlight—shining light everywhere, hoping someone notices. The market doesn't reward flashlights. It rewards lighthouses.

A **lighthouse** doesn't move. It doesn't chase. It stands tall, sending a clear signal—drawing the right ships to it from miles away.

That's what real differentiation looks like. **Not variety. Not flexibility.**

Clarity. Focus. Excellence in one domain.

A Historical Example: In-N-Out Burger

Take In-N-Out Burger. For over 75 years, their menu has stayed astonishingly simple: just burgers, fries, and shakes. No chicken. No salads. No gimmicks.

And yet, they're legendary—with devoted fans willing to drive hours just to eat there (myself included - animal style please).

In-N-Out didn't win by being broad. It won by being **narrow and excellent**, repeatedly. Their focused identity turned them into a magnetic force.

That's the opposite of being a flashlight. That's being a lighthouse.

The Science: Choice Overload and Clarity

This isn't just anecdotal. Cognitive science backs it up. In the iconic "Jam Experiment," researchers Sheena Iyengar (Columbia) and Mark Lepper (Stanford) set up tasting booths in a grocery store:

- One booth offered **24 jam flavors.**
- The other offered just **6 flavors.**

Here's what happened: The booth with 24 options initially drew more interest—but significantly fewer people actually made a purchase compared to the booth with just 6 options. In some cases, **only 3% bought from the large display, while up to 30% bought from the smaller one**—a tenfold difference in conversion likelihood. (stanforddaily.com)

This phenomenon—**choice overload**—shows that too many options paralyze decision-making and reduce action.

Translation for builders: When your positioning is fuzzy—when you're offering "anything anyone needs in construction"—your ideal client hesitates. But hone your message, call out your one arena of excellence, and clarity becomes magnetic.

> ⌐▶ **Real Talk:** When you're a flashlight, you're forgettable. When you're a lighthouse, you're magnetic.

The Sea of One

Imagine standing in a crowded harbor. Hundreds of boats, all with their lights on, all yelling for attention. That is what the construction market feels like when you are bidding on everything, chasing everyone, and hoping someone notices you. Now imagine you are the only lighthouse on the shoreline. No shouting. No chasing. Just a steady, clear signal. That is the power of positioning yourself in a **Sea of One.**

A Sea of One means you deliberately choose to:

- Serve the clients you want, not the ones you tolerate.
- Take the projects that align with your strengths and profitability.
- Craft a message so distinct that when people think about building in your niche, your name is the only one that comes to mind.

This strategy becomes your economic engine, allowing you to focus resources on the type of projects that generate the highest gross margins. By honing in on a single project type where your skills shine, such as custom lakefront homes or upscale urban developments, you not only increase efficiency but also elevate the profitability of each job. Analyze your past projects to uncover which types delivered the best margins and repeat those successes.

Tyler's Transformation

Tyler was a custom builder in Florida, doing about $4 million a year. On paper, it looked good. In reality, he was a mess. He said yes to everything — a $100K deck here, a $750K spec home there, a $2M custom if he was lucky. His weeks were chaos. His profits were unpredictable. And his stress level was through the roof.

When we mapped his projects on the **Genius Model** (profitable, enjoyable, desired), the truth smacked him in the face: most of his jobs were in the "grind" category. Low-margin, high-hassle work that kept him busy but broke.

So we made the call: **no more projects under $1M.**

He focused his brand and messaging around *signature custom lakefront homes.* We helped him refine his proposals, differentiate himself, and communicate his value with confidence.

Here's what happened in 12 months:

- Revenue grew from **$4M → $8M.**
- Average project size doubled.
- Gross margins increased by **6 points.**
- Instead of 14 scattered jobs, he managed 7 focused, profitable builds.
- And for the first time in years, he took a 2-week-long vacation without a single job blowing up.

Tyler didn't work harder. He didn't add more hours. He simply stopped being a flashlight and became a lighthouse.

Differentiation created demand. And demand created freedom.

The framework is simple:

1. Get crystal clear on **who you serve.**
2. Plant your flag with **differentiation.**
3. Build systems that make you **magnetic.**

This isn't about doing more. It's about doing less — on purpose — so your business becomes the lighthouse everyone can see.

The Project Audit Exercise

Differentiation isn't theory — it's math. You don't need a 90-page business plan to find your niche. You need a simple audit of the work you're already doing.

Here's the exercise I give my clients. Grab a sheet of paper (or a whiteboard if you think better standing up) and make three columns:

1. **Profitable** – Which projects actually made you money? Not "looked good on paper" but left cash in the bank.

2. **Enjoyable** – Which projects didn't drain you? Think about the clients, the trades, the process. Did you actually like building it? Were the clients fun? Did they send their equally awesome friends to you?

3. **Desired** – Which projects would you want more of in the future? These are the jobs that build your brand, are in demand in your market, and attract the right clients - the ultimate combo.

Now, list every project from the last 12–18 months into those columns. Be brutally honest.

- Some projects will hit one column.
- A few will hit two.
- And maybe one or two will hit all three.

Those projects — the ones that score **Profitable + Enjoyable + Desired** — that's your **sweet spot.**

That's where your niche lives.

Next Step

Circle the projects in your sweet spot. Ask yourself:

- How do I show more of these in my marketing? How can I ensure that Mrs. Smith sees my material and *knows* I'm the only choice?
- How can I position myself so that these are the only calls I receive? How do I structure my lead flow so that non-fits self-disqualify?

- What would happen if I said *no* to everything outside of this circle for the next 12 months? What would my profits look like? My sanity? My life?

That's how you stop being a flashlight. That's how you become a lighthouse.

The Doorway to Lead Flow

Once you've defined your niche and established your differentiation, everything changes.

Marketing stops feeling like begging.

Sales stops feeling like chasing.

And the right clients start finding you, rather than the other way around.

> └▶ **Real Talk:** Differentiation is the **gateway to lead flow.**

Once your market knows *who you are* and *what you stand for*, you can establish a repeatable system to generate high-quality leads — without relying on luck, referrals, or word of mouth.

Lever 1 makes you a lighthouse.

Lever 2 builds the engine that draws the right ships to your shore.

And that's where we go next.

Your Hidden Bonus Awaits

Every chapter in this book unlocks a deeper level of tools, trainings, and step-by-step guides I normally reserve for private clients. Think of it as the *hidden door* — videos, templates, and frameworks you can put to work today to implement what you're learning.

Scan the QR code if you don't like typing or visit www.builderstimemachine.com/bonus to access it now.

LEVER 2

LEAD FLOW ENGINE

"If you can't describe what you are doing as a process, you don't know what you're doing." – W. Edwards Deming

Busy ≠ Winning

For years, I confused activity with success.

My phone wouldn't stop ringing. My calendar was packed. My inbox looked like a war zone. I told myself, *"I must be doing something right — look how busy I am."*

But here's what I didn't realize: half of those calls were from people who would never hire me. The other half weren't ready for months — sometimes years.

I wasn't running a business. I was running a lottery booth. Hoping the next phone call, the next email, the next referral would be the winning ticket.

That's how most builders operate today. Their entire pipeline depends on chance: a referral here, a random inquiry there, perhaps a realtor sending a lead occasionally.

The problem? Hope is not a lead flow strategy.

> ⌐▶ **Real Talk:** If you want consistent growth, you need a **Lead Flow Engine** — a system that produces opportunities predictably, not sporadically.

Referrals Aren't a Business Plan

When I work with builders who "worked off referrals for years", I ask a simple question. "That's great!", I say... "How many will you have next month so we can plan?". Crickets...

For decades, builders have been taught to treat referrals like gold. And don't get me wrong—referrals are wonderful. They feel warm, easy, almost effortless. The problem is, they're also unreliable. A referral isn't a system. It's a gamble.

History repeatedly proves this point. In the 1930s, Hollywood movie studios discovered something fascinating: one ad wasn't enough to get people into theaters. People had to see the same poster, the same tagline, the same film promotion multiple times before they finally made the decision to buy a ticket. In fact, the studios realized it often took **seven different exposures** to drive a single purchase. That discovery became known as the **Rule of 7**, and it has guided marketers ever since. ("The Marketing Rule of 7", n.d.)

And in today's world? The noise has multiplied a thousand times. A single ad or one random referral rarely sticks. Some modern advertisers suggest it takes not seven, but **20 or more touchpoints** before a buyer makes a move. ("How Many Marketing Touchpoints Convert A Lead?", 2025) In other words, being seen once or twice isn't even close to enough.

Science backs this up. Psychologist Robert Zajonc demonstrated what's called the **mere exposure effect**—the simple idea that the more often we see something, the more we tend to like and trust it. ("Robert Zajonc - Wikipedia", n.d.)

People gravitate toward the familiar. Later research showed why: repeated exposure makes the brain's job easier. Psychologists refer to this as "processing fluency." When something is easy for the brain to recognize and understand, it feels safe. And when it feels safe, it feels good. ("Processing fluency", n.d.)

This is where referrals break down. A referral is one exposure, maybe two. But what happens when that client sees three other builders more often than they see you? Their brain tags *those* builders as familiar, safe, and trustworthy—even if you're the better choice.

The bottom line is this: if your entire business development strategy depends on referrals, you're fishing in the world's smallest pool. You're waiting on a chance. You're gambling on the 3% of people who happen to be ready to buy right now, and hoping that when they finally are, someone mentions your name at the exact right moment.

> ⌐▶ **Real Talk:** That's not a business plan. That's roulette.

Real businesses understand that lead flow is about **intentionally engaging 100% of the market**:

- The 3% who are ready to move now.
- The 7% who are almost ready.
- And the 90% who aren't ready yet—but will be someday—or may tell a friend who is.

If you build your system to show up repeatedly, with clarity and value, you don't just hope for referrals. You become the familiar, trusted lighthouse your clients can't ignore when it's time to build.

The Layered Lead Flow Ecosystem

So if referrals alone won't get you there, what will?

The answer is a **Lead Flow Engine**—a system that doesn't rely on luck, timing, or someone else remembering your name. A true engine pulls in opportunities at every stage of the buyer journey, so your pipeline is never empty, and you're never left hoping for the next phone call.

Here's how it works.

The market isn't one big pool of people waiting to hire a builder. It's three very different groups:

- A small slice—maybe **3% of people—are ready to build right now.** These are the ones everyone is chasing. They're the "low-hanging fruit," and you should absolutely capture them.

- Another group—about **7%—is almost ready.** They're researching, saving, talking with their spouse, looking at lots, sketching ideas. They're close, but they're not pulling the trigger today.

- And then there's the vast majority—**the other 90%.** They're dreaming, watching, waiting. They don't even know if building is possible for them yet. But here's the thing: every year, a percentage of that 90% moves into the "ready" group.

> ⌐⋯▶ **Real Talk:** Most builders only talk to the 3%. That's why they're always in feast-or-famine mode.

But the smart ones? They build a layered ecosystem that touches all three groups:

1. **Attract the Ready Now.** You achieve this through marketing that grabs attention—ads, some SEO, direct outreach, clear messaging, networking, clubs and associations, and more. It's the front door of your engine. You capture the people already looking.

2. **Nurture the Almost Ready.** This is where most builders drop the ball. They meet someone who isn't ready today, and then they vanish. But with the right nurture system—emails that take them on a specific journey, retargeting, helpful check-ins—you stay in front of them until the timing is right.

3. **Stay Visible to the Not Yet.** This is the long game. Content, social proof, market presence, long tail nurture sequences. It's not about closing them tomorrow. It's about being the only name they trust when they finally decide to build. It's about capturing every lead that comes into your world whether in-person, through your website or otherwise, and sending them on a very purposeful journey, one that can last years, and ends with money in your bank account and another happy client.

When you put all three layers together, you stop being the flashlight, hoping your random beam happens to hit the right person at the right time. You become the lighthouse that's always shining—visible, consistent, magnetic.

That's the essence of the Lead Flow Engine: turning randomness into reliability.

From Dead Leads to Closed Jobs

One of my clients came to our kickoff call frustrated. He was earning about $6 million a year, but every project came from referrals. When the referrals slowed, so did the business. Revenue down - stress way up. His pipeline looked like a flatline—random spikes of opportunity followed by weeks of silence.

When we pulled his CRM (you do have a CRM, right?), he had **hundreds of "dead" leads**—people who had inquired, taken a call, even received estimates, but never moved forward. He had written them off as wasted time.

Instead of chasing new referrals, we built a **layered lead flow engine** around those old contacts. We put them into a simple nurture campaign—value-driven emails, a few targeted ads, and personal follow-ups. Nothing complicated. Just consistent touches that kept him top of mind.

Here's what happened in 90 days:

- **4 old leads came back to life and signed contracts, or sent friends and family who did.**

- His average project size increased because those who circled back were more financially prepared.

- And most importantly, his mindset shifted. He realized he didn't need to wait around for the phone to ring. He had control. This - more than the revenue - was worth the exercise.

By the end of the year, those "dead" leads had generated over **$2M in revenue**—without a single new referral —on a list that was previously considered "dead".

That's the power of building an engine. It eliminates the randomness from your business and replaces it with something predictable, repeatable, and scalable.

Map Your Lead Sources & Scoring

If you want to build a Lead Flow Engine, you need to know two things:

1. **Where are your leads really coming from?**
2. **Which ones are worth your time?**

Most builders I meet can't answer with confidence. They'll say, "Oh, most of our business comes from referrals," but when we dig deeper, it turns out half their "referrals" started with a Google search or drove by a jobsite sign, mentioned them to a friend - and the friend sent them along. The truth is fuzzy, and when the truth is fuzzy, you can't build a system.

Here's a simple exercise to get clarity:

Step 1: Map Your Sources

Pull every lead from the last 12 months. Then categorize them by source. Typical buckets look like this:

- Referrals (clients, subs, realtors, friends)
- Website/SEO
- Paid ads
- Social media

- Jobsite signs
- Events or networking

Be honest. Guessing isn't good enough. If you don't know, start asking every new lead, "How did you hear about us?"

∟⋯▶ **Real Talk:** Also ask, "Why did you choose to call us and why now?"... the "why now, why me" question is a sales tactic in disguise... it starts the conversation with them telling you why they sold themselves on calling you...before you ever open your mouth. It's strategic positioning 101, and we'll dive deeper on this (and what to do with that info to get them across the finish line) in upcoming chapters.

Step 2: Score the Quality

Not all leads are created equal. Some are dream clients, others are tire-kickers. Score each lead using a simple scale from 1–3:

- **3 = High-quality.** Ready, qualified, and profitable.
- **2 = Medium-quality.** Interested but not quite ready or not an ideal fit.
- **1 = Low-quality.** Wasting time, wrong budget, wrong project.

Step 3: Look for Patterns

Now connect the dots. Which sources produced the most "3s"? Which sources filled your pipeline with "1s"?

This is where the lightbulb goes off. You'll see that certain sources consistently feed you profitable projects—and others are just noise.

Step 4: Double Down & Automate

Once you know the truth, you can:

- Invest more in the sources that deliver 3s.
- Automate nurture campaigns for the 2s.
- Eliminate or delegate the 1s so they stop draining your time. *Hint: We'll keep them on your list until they unsubscribe, because sending 10 emails costs the same as sending 1,000 in most cases. This is one instance when a wider net could possibly serve you well in the future.*

This is the foundation of your Lead Flow Engine: clarity on what's working, discipline to double down, and structure to keep the almost-ready leads warm until they're ready to sign.

From Flow to Fit

When you build a true Lead Flow Engine, the anxiety fades. You're no longer waiting on the phone to ring or crossing your fingers for referrals. You know where your next opportunities are coming from, because you've built a system that attracts them.

But more leads aren't the ultimate goal. **The right leads are.**

If you don't have a way to filter, qualify, and convert, an overflowing pipeline can become just as exhausting as an empty one. You'll spend hours chasing bad fits, wasting time estimating, and discounting your value.

That's why once you've built your engine, the next lever becomes critical: **Premium Client Conversion.**

Because it's not enough to get more at-bats. You have to step up to the plate knowing you're only swinging at the right pitches.

That's where we go next.

PS - If you want to dive deeper, I have a private training called "Fast and Slow Leads" that you can go watch right now.

Your Hidden Bonus Awaits

Every chapter in this book unlocks a deeper level of tools, trainings, and step-by-step guides I normally reserve for private clients. Think of it as the *hidden door* — videos, templates, and frameworks you can put to work today to implement what you're learning.

Scan the QR code if you don't like typing or visit www.builderstimemachine.com/bonus to access it now.

LEVER 3

PREMIUM CLIENT CONVERSION

"The difference between successful people and really successful people is that really successful people say no to almost everything."
– Warren Buffett

Stop Chasing, Start Choosing

I'll never forget the year I submitted **42 bids** and won less than a quarter of them. At first, I thought the answer was to hustle harder—bid faster, bid more, sharpen my pencil, and "be competitive."

But all that really meant was more late nights, more unpaid hours, and more time chasing clients who were never going to choose me in the first place.

That's the trap most builders fall into. They mistake activity for control. They think if they just bid enough jobs, eventually the right ones will land. But in reality, they're playing the client's game, not their own.

Every hour you spend chasing a bad fit is an hour you could've spent building trust with the right one. And the right one doesn't want the cheapest builder. They want the most aligned builder. The one who understands their vision, values, and expectations.

> ⌐▶ **Real Talk:** You don't need *more* clients. You need the **right clients.**

And the shift begins with how you think about conversion.

Sales Isn't Pressure, It's Filtering

Most builders hate the word "sales." It feels slimy, like you're manipulating someone into buying something they don't want. So they avoid it. They send out bids, cross their fingers, and tell themselves: *"If the price is right, the client will choose us."*

But sales done right isn't pressure. It's not about convincing. It's about filtering.

The best builders don't try to win every project. They build a process that separates the clients who are a great fit from the ones who will drain their time, margin, and sanity. It's not about closing harder. It's about qualifying smarter.

History proves this point.

In the early 1900s, Harry Selfridge, founder of Selfridges department store in London, changed retail forever with one phrase: *"The customer is always right."* He didn't mean every customer should be catered to at all costs. What he understood was that the right customer—the one aligned with the store's values, expectations, and positioning—would fuel growth for decades. Selfridge filtered by creating an experience that appealed to a specific type of client: aspirational, fashionable, and status-conscious. His competitors, trying to please everyone, drowned in discount wars. Sound familiar?

Science backs it up, too.

In a Harvard Business Review study on customer profitability, researchers found that not all customers contribute equally. In fact, a small percentage often accounts for the majority of profit, while others destroy value. The takeaway? Treating all prospects as equal is a fast track to mediocrity. The winners design systems that attract and retain their "ideal" clients while politely filtering out the rest (HBR, *Managing Customer Profitability*, 1997). (Kaplan, 2001)

And behavioral science adds another layer. Studies on **choice overload**—like the famous Jam Experiment by Iyengar and Lepper at Stanford—show that people make better, faster decisions when they have fewer, clearer options. When you position yourself as the obvious choice for a very specific client, you don't just win more business—you make it easier for the right clients to choose you.

⌐…▶ **Real Talk:** Sales isn't about trying to get everyone to say yes. It's about building a system where only the right people get through the door in the first place.

When you stop chasing every project and start filtering for alignment, two things happen. Your close rate skyrockets. And your stress plummets.

The Premium Path

If sales is really filtering, then the obvious question becomes: *How do you build the filter?*

The answer is what I call the **Premium Path**—a simple process that positions you as the trusted guide and ensures only the right clients move forward. Think of it as the opposite of a revolving door. It's a funnel that narrows, clarifies, and qualifies.

Here's how it works.

Step 1: Positioning Before the Pitch

Before you ever sit down with a prospect, they should already know who you are, what you stand for, and what you don't do. This comes from your marketing, your messaging, your sales process and your presence in the market. If your brand screams "We'll build anything for anyone," you've already lost. The Premium Path starts with authority—showing up as the builder who owns one clear space in the market.

Step 2: Pre-Qualification

Once someone raises their hand, don't jump straight to bidding. Instead, filter. A simple intake process—budget ranges, timeline, project type, expectations—immediately separates the serious clients from the time-wasters. This isn't about being rude; it's about respect. Respect for your time, your team's time, and the client's. It's why I urge ALL of my builder clients to work from a paid design agreement - there is no better filter in the world than the customer having to put some of their money on the line.

Step 3: The Conversion Conversation

By the time you're actually sitting down face-to-face, you're not "selling" anymore. You're confirming alignment. You've already made it clear what you do, how you work, and what kind of clients you're best for. They've gone on a very specific customer journey. Now, you're simply deciding if this project and this client are the right fit for both sides. That shift—from chasing to choosing—changes everything.

When you put the Premium Path in place, something remarkable happens: you stop competing on price. The tire-kickers, the bargain-hunters, the misaligned clients—they never make it through the filter. And the ones who do? They're the ones who already see your value, trust your process, and want to pay for it.

That's the power of the Premium Path. It doesn't just help you close more business. It helps you close the *right* business.

From Bidding Wars to Selective Wins

One of my clients, a builder in OK, was doing about $8M a year. On the surface, he looked successful. Behind the scenes, he was drowning in paperwork, a glorified admin in his own company.

Every week, his desk was stacked with bid requests—ten, fifteen, sometimes twenty at a time. Nights and weekends disappeared into estimating: chasing subs, plugging numbers, revising spreadsheets. Yet less than one in five ever turned into a contract. Four out of five times, all that effort was wasted.

When he came to me, his conclusion was the same one I hear from builders everywhere: *"I need to hire an estimator."*

But that wasn't the real problem. That was just the surface symptom.

This is where we used the **Toyota "5 Whys" process**—a simple tool for diagnosing problems by asking "why" until you reach the root cause.

- **Why** do you need an estimator?
- Because I have too many estimates to get out.
- **Why** do you have too many estimates?
- Because every prospect who asks for one gets one.
- **Why** does every prospect get one?
- Because I don't have a system to qualify them first.
- **Why** don't you qualify them first?
- Because I'm afraid if I don't bid, I'll lose the job.

- **Why** do you think bidding equals winning?
- Because that's how the industry has always done it.

By the time we hit the fifth "why," the problem was clear: he didn't need an estimator. He needed a filter. Out of 20 estimates, maybe 4 were even a realistic fit—and of those, only 2–3 would ever move forward. So why waste precious hours on the other 16?

This is where the **design agreement** became the solution. After we designed his intake process, instead of handing out free hard bids, he introduced a paid pre-construction process. Before he called a single sub or opened another spreadsheet, the client had to commit financially to design and preliminary pricing. That step alone separated the tire-kickers from the serious clients.

The result was dramatic. Within 60 days, his "estimate overload" disappeared. He cut the number of bids in half, but his close rate doubled. Instead of winning 20% of 20 projects, he was winning 40% of 10—and those 10 were better aligned, more profitable, and far less stressful.

└▶ **Real Talk:** Most builders don't have a bidding problem. They have a filtering problem. The real breakthrough comes when you stop asking, *"How do I get all these bids out?"* and start asking, *"Which of these clients are actually worth bidding, and most likely to result in a job won, in the first place?"*

When you solve for that, you don't need an estimator to keep up. You need a process that ensures you only spend time on the high-probability clients—the ones who are serious, committed, and ready to move forward.

Build Your Filters Before You Bid

If you take nothing else from this chapter, take this: **stop giving away bids for free.**

Every hard bid you produce costs time, money, and focus. When you throw them out like candy at a parade, you devalue your expertise and burn out your team. The solution is to build filters—clear checkpoints that ensure only the right clients make it through your process.

Here's how to do it:

Step 1: Diagnose the Real Problem (Toyota's "5 Whys")

When you feel like you "need an estimator," pause. Ask why. Keep asking until you get to the root.

Do you truly need someone to crank out more bids?

Or do you need to stop bidding for people who will never move forward?

Nine times out of ten, it's the second one. Filtering is the cure, not more manpower.

Step 2: Use Pre-Qualification Filters

Before you invest a single minute in a hard bid, require every prospect to go through a short pre-qualification process. Here are five filters I recommend:

1. **Budget Alignment.** "Have you established a budget range for this project?" If their number is 50% below what you build at, you just saved hours.

2. **Timeline.** "When are you hoping to break ground?" If they're still "just looking" for two years from now, you know where to file them.

3. **Project Type.** Does the work fit your specialty? If you're a custom builder, don't waste energy on small renovations for example to "keep the team busy" or "keep cash flow up" - more on this later.

4. **Decision Process.** "Who will be making the final decision?" If there are seven family members involved, expect chaos.

5. **Why Us?** The simplest but most powerful question. If they can't articulate why they want you over anyone else, that's a red flag.

Note: this list is just to get you started. Depending on your business, volume, profit goals and market, we will introduce many other questions at this stage. The important thing is your letting this email/google form/phone call produce enough information that you're crystal clear on whether you should move forward into Step 3.

Step 3: Introduce the Paid Design Agreement

Once a prospect passes your filters, invite them into a **paid pre-construction process.** This is your design agreement. Instead of burning hours chasing sub pricing for free, you provide:

- Preliminary drawings or conceptual layouts.
- Value-engineered options to align vision with budget.
- Rough order-of-magnitude pricing, so they understand feasibility before you hard bid.
- An allotment of interior design and selections hours.

This shifts the dynamic. You're no longer "one of many" builders handing out free estimates—you're a trusted advisor guiding the client's vision and understand the value of both your expertise and your time. And because they've invested money, they're invested in the relationship.

Step 4: Protect Your Time & Team

By implementing filters and a design agreement, you reduce your bid load dramatically. You no longer need an estimator just to keep up with a flood of unqualified requests. Instead, every hour you and your team spend is focused on high-probability clients—the 20% of opportunities that lead to 80% of your revenue.

When you filter first, you stop reacting and start choosing. You eliminate the noise. And the clients who remain are not just more likely to move forward—they're more likely to value your process, respect your expertise, and pay for it.

That's how you escape the bidding trap.

From Clients to Capacity

When you stop chasing and start filtering, your business changes.

You're no longer buried under bids you'll never win.

You're no longer negotiating with bargain hunters who don't respect your time.

Instead, you're sitting across the table from clients who have already chosen you in their mind before the contract is signed. Clients who value your expertise, trust your process, and are willing to invest in it.

But here's the catch: when you start converting premium clients, a new challenge appears.

Premium clients expect premium delivery. They want clarity, professionalism, and consistency at every step—from design to punch list. And if your business is still running on duct tape and heroics, you'll quickly find yourself maxed out again, just in a different way.

That's why the next law is critical. You can't scale premium clients without a premium team.

Law 2 is about **The Machine**—building the structure, roles, and systems that let your business deliver at a higher level without you being the bottleneck.

∟⋯▶ **Real Talk:** If we installed the systems to get you 10 more projects tomorrow - what would break next?

Because it's one thing to win better clients.

It's another thing to build a company that can actually serve them well.

And that's where we go next.

Your Hidden Bonus Awaits

Every chapter in this book unlocks a deeper level of tools, trainings, and step-by-step guides I normally reserve for private clients. Think of it as the *hidden door* — videos, templates, and frameworks you can put to work today to implement what you're learning.

Scan the QR code if you don't like typing or visit
www.builderstimemachine.com/bonus to access it now.

LAW 2

THE MACHINE

Winning attention is one thing. Delivering consistently at scale is another.

Most builders don't stall because of marketing. They stall because their business can't carry the weight of the opportunities they've created.

That's where **The Machine** comes in.

The Machine is the infrastructure of your business—the structure, leadership, and culture that allow growth to compound instead of collapse. Without it, every new client feels heavier, every new project more chaotic. With it, scale becomes sustainable.

I've seen too many talented builders hit a ceiling not because demand dried up, but because their company was still duct-taped together with spreadsheets, late-night texts, and the owner making every decision. At $2M, that feels heroic. At $10M, it feels impossible.

> ⌐▶ **Real Talk:** What got you here won't get you there.

The same hustle that once fueled your success will strangle you if you try to scale without structure.

That's why The Machine matters. It's the shift from *you being the hub of the wheel* to building a company that runs without you at the center.

In the chapters ahead, we'll cover three levers that bring The Machine to life:

- **Structured for Scale** – how to escape the hub-and-spoke trap and build an org chart that carries the weight.

- **Team Leadership** – how to stop blaming "bad hires" and start multiplying results through clarity, cadence, and coaching.

- **Culture by Design** – how to create an environment where the right people thrive, the wrong ones self-select out, and your values get lived out daily.

Because here's the reality: you don't just need more clients. You need a business that can handle them.

You don't just need more projects. You need a machine that can deliver them—profitably, predictably, and without grinding you into dust.

The Magnet gets you noticed.

The Machine keeps you standing.

Now, let's build it.

LEVER 4

STRUCTURED FOR SCALE

"The strength of the team is each individual member. The strength of each member is the team." – Phil Jackson

The Hub-and-Spoke Trap

If you've ever felt like the hub of a wheel—with every decision, every question, every problem running through you—you're not alone.

Most builders operate exactly like that. At $2M or $3M a year, it feels manageable. You're hustling hard, but you can keep up. At $5M, it gets heavy. By $10M, it's unbearable.

Note: these are national averages, but it's the same at $4M or $14M or $40M depending on your market.

This is what I call the **hub-and-spoke trap.** You, the owner, are the hub. Your team, your subs, your clients—they're the spokes. And every day, all the weight of communication, coordination, and decision-making comes through you. The leader with 1000 helpers.

> ⌐⋯➤ **Real Talk:** A wheel like that can't spin forever. Eventually, the hub cracks. It's not if... it's when.

I've watched builder after builder stall out—not because of lack of talent, not because of lack of demand, but because their company was missing the one ingredient that makes scale possible: structure.

The ceiling you're hitting isn't about spreadsheets, or software, or "working harder." It's about building a machine that can run without you being the axle holding everything together.

Scale Isn't Spreadsheets- It's Structure

Most builders believe they can muscle their way to growth with better tools—new spreadsheets, fancier project management software, or more hours at the office. But spreadsheets don't scale. People and structure do.

History proves it.

In the 1920s, **Alfred Sloan took over General Motors** when it was on the brink of collapse. Ford was dominating the market with the Model T, while GM was a messy collection of competing divisions. Sloan didn't outwork Ford. He didn't invent better spreadsheets. He created **structure.**

He introduced the modern divisional org chart—separating GM into clear business units (Chevrolet, Buick, Cadillac), each with its own leadership, accountability, and profit responsibility. That one move allowed GM to scale rapidly, adapt to market changes, and ultimately overtake Ford as the world's largest automaker. Structure beat hustle.

Science backs this up.

A **Harvard Business School study on organizational design** found that companies with clearly defined roles and accountability systems grew revenue **30% faster** and were significantly more resilient during downturns compared to companies that relied on ad-hoc leadership (HBS Working Paper, *The Performance Effects of Organizational Design*, 2018).

And neuroscience adds another layer: studies on **decision fatigue** show that the more decisions an individual makes in a day, the lower the quality of those decisions becomes. (Baumeister, 1998) When the owner is the hub making every call, they're not just slowing growth— they're actively degrading the company's performance.

> ⌐▶ **Real Talk:** Scale isn't about doing more. It's about designing a machine that does more without you.

Structure creates capacity. Capacity creates freedom. And freedom is the real currency of scale.

The Org Chart Ladder

If structure is the key to scale, the question becomes: *what does the right structure look like?*

Most builders resist org charts because they feel corporate, stiff, or unnecessary. But the truth is, an org chart isn't about bureaucracy—it's about clarity. It's the map that shows who owns what, so you don't end up owning everything.

I call this the **Org Chart Ladder**—the natural progression most builders go through as they grow (again - figures are relative to your market - but the lesson remains):

Step 1: Chaos (Owner Does Everything)

At $1M–$2M, it's just you and maybe a helper, an admin, a super. You're selling, estimating, managing, swinging a hammer, and answering the phone. It's survival mode. No real structure, just grit.

Step 2: Delegation by Task (Owner as Hub)

At $3M–$5M, you've added a few roles—maybe an admin, a dedicated superintendent, or a project manager. But you're still the hub. Everyone reports to you. Every decision runs through you. You're less on the jobsite, but you're more in your inbox.

Step 3: Defined Roles (Owner as Leader)

At $6M–$10M, structure becomes essential. Instead of tasks floating around, roles are clearly defined: sales, estimating, operations, finance, client care. Each has an owner, and accountability is clear. The business no longer depends on you being everywhere at once and available 24 hours a day.

Step 4: Leadership Layer (Owner as CEO)

Beyond $10M, you add a leadership team. Now you're not just delegating tasks—you're delegating outcomes. Your project managers manage, your estimator estimates, your ops leader runs production. You shift from operator to strategic leader, working *on* the business instead of *in* it.

Step 5: Scalable Machine (Owner as Visionary)

At $20M and beyond, the business runs as a machine. You set vision and direction, your leadership team drives execution, and the org chart carries the weight. You're no longer the hub—you're the lighthouse guiding the company forward.

The Org Chart Ladder isn't about titles or hierarchy. It's about freedom. Every rung you climb takes weight off your shoulders and puts it where it belongs—onto a structure designed to carry it.

Without it, growth becomes chaos. With it, growth becomes scale.

Throwing Bodies at Problems: The Silent Killer of Business Growth

Every builder I know has hit that wall: jobs are stacking up, deadlines are looming, and the knee-jerk solution feels obvious—hire more people. More hands, lighter work... right?

Not so fast.

In twenty years of advising construction businesses, I can tell you this reflex is one of the most expensive mistakes you can make.

> ⌐▶ **Real Talk:** Adding bodies to a broken system doesn't fix the problem—it multiplies it.

I've watched owners go from managing five employees with manageable stress to managing fifteen and drowning—with no real increase in profit. All they bought themselves was more headaches, more complexity, and less time to think.

Construction is especially vulnerable to this trap. Unlike a software company, we can't just flip a switch and scale without people. Every job needs boots on the ground, hands on tools, eyes on details. That makes it *really* tempting to believe every challenge can be solved by hiring another estimator, project manager, or super. But if your foundation is cracked, all you're doing is building a bigger house on top of it. It crumbles. Every time.

Think about it:

- If your estimating process is flawed, hiring three more estimators just multiplies the flaws.
- If your project management is fuzzy on accountability, ten PMs just create ten different versions of confusion.

The math is brutal, and yet I see builders repeat it every day.

And worse? You, the owner, pay the steepest price.

Every hire needs training, attention, and management. Before long, you're not running your business—you're babysitting it. I've sat across from countless builders who dreamed of freedom but accidentally built themselves a cage.

This chapter is about breaking that cycle.

We're going to dig into three things:

1. **The hidden cost of panic hiring.** Not just the payroll numbers, but the toll it takes on your energy, culture, and sanity.

2. **Why fit beats force.** How to match people to their natural wiring (instead of forcing square pegs into round holes) and how that shift changes everything.

3. **A roadmap for strategic staffing.** How to grow your team in a way that adds capacity instead of consuming it.

Make no mistake: you need people to grow. Good people. But there's a world of difference between hiring strategically and hiring desperately. One creates leverage. The other creates liability.

When you apply these principles, you stop seeing employees as costs and start seeing them as assets. You'll know when to hire, who to hire, and—just as important—when hiring isn't the answer at all.

That's how you stop throwing bodies at problems and finally create the space to lead like a CEO, not babysit like a superintendent.

From Stalled at $6M to Scaling Past $12M

I worked with a builder in CA who had been stuck in the **$5–6M range for years.** He was talented, his projects were beautiful, and demand wasn't the issue. The bottleneck was him.

Every sub wanted his approval. Every client wanted his reassurance. Every team member needed his sign-off. He was the hub, and the spokes were pulling him apart.

On the surface, it looked like he needed more people—another project manager, maybe a second designer. But when we dug in, the problem wasn't headcount. It was structure.

He had talented people on his team, but none of them had clear ownership. Roles overlapped, accountability was hazy, and in the end, everything funneled back to his desk.

So we mapped his **Org Chart Ladder.** We didn't add bodies. We added clarity.

One PM owned scheduling. Another owned client communication. Estimating had a single point of accountability. Finance was pulled out of his inbox and given to his admin with a proper process.

The results were immediate. Clients started going directly to the right person instead of always circling back to the owner. Subs got clear answers faster. Projects flowed smoother. Change orders slowed and the ones he did have were signed off on and implemented easily.

Within 18 months, revenue had doubled—from $6M to over $12M— without him working more hours. In fact, he was working less. The weight shifted from his shoulders to the structure and allowed him to do what he did best - grow the business.

That's the power of structure. It doesn't just enable growth—it makes growth sustainable. Without it, you'll stall. With it, you can finally scale.

Draft Your Future Org & Accountability Chart

If you don't design your structure, it will design itself. And that "default org chart" usually looks like chaos—everyone doing a little bit of everything, and the owner stuck in the middle.

The way out is to design your org chart *before* you need it. Don't think about who you have today. Think about the company you're building 18–24 months from now.

Here's how to start:

Step 1: Sketch the Future Org Chart

- Put **you** at the top—not as "doer of everything," but as **CEO/Visionary.**

- Create the key functions every construction company needs:

  - **Sales/Marketing** – generating and converting leads (this should be one of the last things you outsource - more on this later).

  - **Estimating/Pre-Con** – pricing, design agreements and contracts, sub and bid management.

  - **Operations** – project management, design, scheduling, client care, warranty, etc.

  - **Finance/Admin** – invoicing, AR/AP, reporting, permits, social media, calendar management, etc

- Under each function, write the **role titles** you'll eventually need (Project Manager, Estimator, Client Care Coordinator, Controller, etc.).

Step 2: Assign Accountability

For each function, ask: *Who owns the outcome?*

- It doesn't matter if that person has help or support—what matters is that one name is ultimately accountable.
- Example: If "Operations" is everyone's responsibility, it's no one's responsibility. Make it clear.

Step 3: Compare to Today

Now overlay your current team. Who's already filling those seats? Where are the gaps? Where are you wearing three hats?

This gap analysis gives you a **hiring roadmap.** It shows you the next critical roles to fill—not just based on "pain today," but based on the structure you're building toward.

Step 4: Communicate & Implement

Don't hide this chart in a drawer. Share it with your team. Let them see the bigger picture. It creates clarity, reduces friction, and shows them a future they can grow into.

└┄▶ **Real Talk:** An org chart isn't a piece of paper. It's a **decision-making tool.** It tells your team who owns what, so they stop defaulting everything back to you.

When you design your structure in advance, you get ahead of the growth curve. You stop being the hub, and you start being the leader of a machine that can run without you.

From Structure to Strength

When you finally step out of the hub-and-spoke trap and build a real structure, everything changes.

You're no longer the bottleneck. Your team knows who owns what. Clients get answers without waiting on you. Subs move faster because decisions don't sit in your inbox for days.

But structure alone isn't enough. A chart on a wall won't magically create accountability or drive results. That takes leadership.

Once the seats are defined, the real question becomes: *how do you get the right people in those seats, and how do you lead them well?*

That's where the next lever comes in—**Team Leadership.**

Because even the best-designed org chart will collapse without the right people owning their roles and pulling in the same direction.

In the next chapter, we'll shift from **designing the machine** to **powering the machine.** We'll look at how to inspire, direct, and develop your team so the structure doesn't just exist—it thrives.

I'll also introduce you to The Crystal Ball - the secret weapon that companies like IBM and NASA use to predict who is best for what seat - and how you can use it to eliminate wasted time, money and stress on bad hires before they ever step foot on the job.

Your Hidden Bonus Awaits

Every chapter in this book unlocks a deeper level of tools, trainings, and step-by-step guides I normally reserve for private clients. Think of it as the *hidden door* — videos, templates, and frameworks you can put to work today to implement what you're learning.

Scan the QR code if you don't like typing or visit www.builderstimemachine.com/bonus to access it now.

TEAM LEADERSHIP

"There are no bad teams, only bad leaders."
– Jocko Willink

Why Builders Fail Isn't What You Think

Most builders think they struggle because they don't have the right people. They blame a superintendent who can't keep up, a project manager who misses details, or an admin who drops the ball.

> ⌐▶ **Real Talk:** Nine times out of ten, the problem isn't the people. It's the leadership.

You can have talented players on the field, but without a clear playbook and a coach who keeps them aligned, they'll always underperform. They're not bad people—they're under-led people.

I've seen builders hire, fire, and rehire the same roles over and over, always convinced they just "can't find good help." But the pattern never changes. Why? Because the team doesn't need more control. They need more clarity, consistency, and coaching.

It's like the lady with 5 ex husbands who "were all jerks"... there is always a common denominator.

Leadership is the multiplier. Get it wrong, and you burn through people, profits, and patience. Get it right, and even an average team can deliver extraordinary results.

Leadership Isn't Control, It's Clarity and Alignment

Most owners secretly believe that leadership means control. If they could just watch closer, double-check more details, or tighten their grip, things would finally get done right.

But the best leaders don't succeed by controlling more. They succeed by aligning more.

History proves this point.

When **Dwight D. Eisenhower** led the Allied forces in World War II, he wasn't the smartest tactician in the room—he had generals like Patton and Montgomery for that. His genius wasn't control. It was alignment. Eisenhower created clarity of mission, established a cadence of communication, and empowered each general to execute in their own way. That's how the most complex military operation in history—D-Day—succeeded. One leader aligned thousands, without trying to control every move.

Science backs it up.

In a **Gallup study on employee engagement**, the #1 driver of high performance wasn't perks or pay—it was clarity. Employees who strongly agreed they knew what was expected of them were **2.8x more likely** to be engaged at work (Gallup, *State of the American Workplace*, 2017).

And research in organizational psychology shows that teams with consistent alignment rituals—weekly check-ins, shared scorecards, and feedback loops—deliver significantly higher output with less friction (Harvard Business Review, *The Power of Small Wins*, Amabile & Kramer, 2011).

> ⌐▶ **Real Talk:** Leadership isn't about holding tighter—it's about creating clarity, cadence, and alignment so your team can move faster without you micromanaging.

The stronger your grip, the weaker your team becomes. But the clearer your leadership, the stronger your team performs.

The 3Cs of Leadership

If leadership isn't about control, then what is it about?

Working with builders from $3M to $30M, from Vancouver to Miami, I've found that great leadership comes down to **three simple levers**—what we call the **3Cs of Leadership**:

1. Clarity

Your team should never wonder: *What's expected of me?*

- Clear roles → defined on the org chart.
- Clear goals → measurable targets, not vague hopes.
- Clear communication → so everyone knows what "done" looks like.

Without clarity, you get chaos. With it, you get alignment.

2. Cadence

Even the clearest goals won't stick if you only talk about them once a year. Leadership is rhythm.

- Weekly team meetings → progress, roadblocks, next steps.
- Daily huddles (for field teams) → short, sharp alignment.
- Quarterly reviews → reflection, correction, direction.

Cadence is what keeps the whole machine moving in sync.

3. Coaching

Leadership isn't just about directing—it's about developing. Your job is to raise the ceiling for your team, not just point at it.

- Coaching questions instead of commands.
- Feedback loops that build people up while holding them accountable.

- Growth plans that turn today's team into tomorrow's leaders.

When you combine **Clarity, Cadence, and Coaching**, something shifts. You stop being the bottleneck, and your team starts carrying the weight. You stop pushing every project forward, and your team starts pulling.

The 3Cs turn leadership from a burden into a multiplier.

From Chaos Meetings to Consistent Leadership Rhythm

One of my clients had grown to about **$19M a year** in revenue. On paper, things looked great. In reality, his office was a revolving door.

Turnover was constant. His project managers were frustrated, his superintendents burned out, and his admin team never seemed to last more than a few months. He thought the problem was hiring. He kept saying, *"I just can't find good people."*

But when I sat in on one of his team meetings, the problem became obvious.

The meeting had no agenda. It started late, wandered in ten directions, and ended with nothing concrete. Half the team left confused, the other half left frustrated. It wasn't a team problem—it was a leadership problem.

We applied the **3Cs.**

First, we created **Clarity**: each role was defined, and every meeting had a clear purpose and outcome.

Next, we installed **Cadence**:

- Mondays were for leadership team check-ins.
- Wednesdays were for project manager huddles.
- Fridays were for field updates and financial scorecards.

Finally, we shifted him into **Coaching mode**: instead of barking out corrections, he started asking questions like, *"What do you need to move this forward?"* and *"What obstacles are in your way?"*

The transformation was dramatic. Within 90 days, turnover slowed. Morale improved. The same people he thought were "bad hires" started performing at a high level. One of his PMs even stepped up into a true leadership role, taking pressure off the owner for the first time in years (he eventually moved into VP of Ops).

Revenue didn't just grow—the **culture stabilized.** And when the culture stabilizes, profit follows.

That's the power of leadership. It's not about finding "better people." It's about becoming a better leader so the people you already have can thrive.

How to Lead with Clarity, Cadence, and Coaching

Leadership can feel abstract until you anchor it into concrete rhythms. Here's how to install the **3Cs of Leadership** inside your building company:

1. Clarity – Define the Game and the Rules

- **Role Descriptions:** Every role gets a one-page description: what they own, what success looks like, who they report to.
- **Scorecard Metrics:** Choose 2–3 numbers each role is accountable for (e.g., PM = % of jobs on schedule, Superintendent = % of punch list items closed on time, etc).
- **Company Goals:** Write down the top 3 quarterly goals on one page. Review them weekly.

When your team knows the game, the rules, and the score, they don't need you to hover.

2. Cadence – Install Rhythms That Drive Momentum

Think of cadence like the heartbeat of your company. Here's a simple system:

- **Daily Huddles (10 minutes max):** Field crews align on safety, tasks, and top priorities.

- **Weekly Meetings (60 minutes):** Leadership or PM team reviews scorecards, tackles issues, assigns next actions.

- **Quarterly Reviews (Half Day):** Step back, review wins, analyze misses, and reset goals.

Consistency matters more than length. A short, sharp weekly meeting done every week beats a rambling "catch-up" once a month.

3. Coaching – Develop People, Don't Just Direct Them

- **Shift from Answers to Questions:** Instead of "Do this." ask *"What's your next step to solve this?"*

- **Feedback Framework:** Use the "SBI model" (Situation–Behavior–Impact) to give feedback that's specific and actionable.

- **Growth Plans:** Meet 1-on-1 quarterly with each key team member. Ask where they want to grow, then create opportunities that stretch them.

Coaching builds leaders, not just workers. And leaders multiply capacity.

Implementation Tip: Start Small

You don't need to roll this out overnight. Start with one rhythm (like a weekly leadership meeting with a scorecard). Once that's solid, add the next. Build the system layer by layer.

> ⌐⋯▶ **Real Talk:** When you combine **Clarity, Cadence, and Coaching**, your leadership stops being reactive and becomes proactive. You stop putting out fires, and your team starts building a rhythm of their own.

From Leadership to Culture

When you put real leadership in place, you feel the shift immediately.

Your meetings run on time. Your team knows what "done" looks like. Problems don't pile up on your desk—they get solved at the right level. For the first time, it feels like the business is moving forward without you dragging it.

But leadership alone isn't the finish line. Leadership creates alignment—but **culture creates momentum.**

Because you can set clear goals and run crisp meetings, but if your team doesn't buy into the deeper values of how you work, and why, cracks will still form. The wrong hire with the wrong attitude can undo six months of progress in six days.

That's why the next lever is **Culture by Design.**

In the next chapter, we'll explore how to build a culture that doesn't just happen by accident, but one that attracts the right people, repels the wrong ones, and reinforces your standards even when you're not in the room. We'll even talk about my secret hiring weapon - I call it The Crystal Ball.

Leadership sets the pace. Culture sets the tone. And when those two align, the machine doesn't just run—it thrives.

Your Hidden Bonus Awaits

Every chapter in this book unlocks a deeper level of tools, trainings, and step-by-step guides I normally reserve for private clients. Think of it as the *hidden door* — videos, templates, and frameworks you can put to work today to implement what you're learning.

Scan the QR code if you don't like typing or visit www.builderstimemachine.com/bonus to access it now.

LEVER 6

CULTURE BY DESIGN

"The culture of any organization is shaped by the worst behavior the leader is willing to tolerate." – Gruenter & Whitaker

Culture by Default vs. Culture by Design

Here's the mistake most builders make: they think culture is something that just "happens." Hire good people, treat them well, and hope for the best.

But culture always exists—whether you design it or not. And if you don't shape it intentionally, it will shape itself, often in ways you don't want.

I once worked with a builder whose projects were gorgeous, margins solid, demand steady—but his team was miserable. Turnover was high. Drama was constant. Subs didn't want to work with them.

Why? Because the culture had been left on autopilot. Gossip spread. Standards slipped. Accountability disappeared. It took a heap of work to turn that ship around… and it didn't have to be that way.

On the flip side, I've seen smaller builders punch way above their weight because their culture was strong. Their people showed up engaged, problems got solved at the lowest level, and clients felt the difference.

> ∟▶ **Real Talk:** Culture eats strategy for breakfast. You can have the best systems and sharpest numbers, but if your culture is toxic, it will eat away at everything you build.

The good news? Culture isn't an accident. It can be designed.

Culture Isn't Perks, It's Standards and Behaviors

Most business owners confuse culture with perks. They think a ping-pong table in the office, Friday pizza lunches, or company swag equals culture. But culture isn't about perks—it's about standards.

Culture is *how people behave when you're not in the room.*

History makes this crystal clear.

When **Herb Kelleher** built Southwest Airlines, he didn't outspend his competitors with fancy lounges or corporate perks. He built a culture around three simple standards: low costs, on-time flights, and fun. That culture wasn't words on a wall—it was behaviors lived out daily, from flight attendants singing safety announcements to employees pitching in to turn planes around faster. The result? For decades,

Southwest was the most consistently profitable airline in the U.S., while bigger airlines with more "perks" struggled.

Science backs it up too.

A **Harvard Business School study on organizational culture** found that companies with strong, intentionally designed cultures outperformed competitors by **20–30% in revenue growth** over a 10-year span (Kotter & Heskett, *Corporate Culture and Performance*, 1992).

And behavioral psychology research shows that **norms drive behavior more than rules**. In experiments, people were far more likely to conform to group norms—even unspoken ones—than to follow written instructions (Cialdini, *Influence*, 2006). Translation? Your people don't rise to the level of what's written in the handbook. They fall to the level of what's tolerated in the culture.

> ⌐▶ **Real Talk:** Culture isn't built on what you preach—it's built on what you permit.

If you don't define and enforce standards, your culture will be defined by the lowest common denominator. But when you intentionally set values, tie them to behaviors, and reinforce them daily, your culture becomes your strongest competitive advantage.

The Culture Blueprint

If culture isn't perks, then how do you actually build it?

The answer is what I call the **Culture Blueprint**—a simple system for turning vague ideas like "values" into daily behaviors your team actually lives.

It's a three-step process: **Values → Standards → Rituals.**

Step 1: Values (Define What You Stand For)

Values are your non-negotiables. They answer the question: *What kind of company are we?*

- Example: Integrity. Excellence. Ownership. Communication.
- But here's the trap—values on their own are just words on a wall.

Step 2: Standards (Translate Values Into Behaviors)

Standards turn values into action. They answer: *What does this value look like in real life?*

- Integrity → We own mistakes immediately and fix them.
- Excellence → Every jobsite is broom-swept at the end of the day.
- Ownership → Problems don't get passed up the chain without at least one proposed solution.
- Communication → Clients get an update every Friday by 5 p.m.

When standards are defined, culture becomes measurable.

Step 3: Rituals (Reinforce the Standards)

Rituals are the habits that keep culture alive. They answer: *How do we make sure this sticks?*

- Weekly team meetings start with a "values in action" story.
- Monthly recognition for team members who lived the standards.
- Quarterly reviews tied not just to performance, but to values alignment.

Values are the *why.*

Standards are the *what.*

Rituals are the *how.*

That's the blueprint. And when you put it in place, culture stops being an accident—it becomes a designed system that reinforces itself day after day.

From Toxic Turnover to a Thriving Culture

I worked with a builder in TX who was doing about **$7M a year** in revenue but constantly felt like he was rebuilding his company from scratch.

Turnover was brutal. Project managers came and went. Admins rarely lasted more than six months. Even some of his best supers eventually burned out. He was convinced the problem was the labor market—"You just can't find good people in this town."

But when I sat with his team, the real problem surfaced. It wasn't pay. It wasn't workload. It was culture.

The company had no clear values, no standards, no rituals. Every day felt reactive. Meetings turned into complaint sessions. Gossip was rampant. Accountability was non-existent. The good people eventually left, and the ones who stayed often made things worse.

We applied the **Culture Blueprint.**

- First, we defined **values** with the leadership team: integrity, ownership, and communication.

- Then, we translated them into **standards.** Integrity meant admitting mistakes immediately. Ownership meant bringing solutions, not just problems. Communication meant Friday updates to every client, no exceptions.

- Finally, we reinforced them with **rituals.** Weekly meetings began with a "values shout-out." Quarterly reviews scored not just performance, but cultural alignment.

The shift was dramatic. Within six months, turnover finally slowed. Within a year, the revolving door had stopped. His team not only stayed, they started policing the culture themselves. Gossip got shut down. Accountability rose. Subs even commented on how different the company "felt" on the jobsite.

Revenue didn't just grow—it grew with less chaos. And the owner no longer felt like he was pushing a boulder uphill alone.

That's the power of culture by design. When you define it, live it, and reinforce it, your company becomes a place where the right people thrive and the wrong people naturally filter out.

How to Build Culture That Sticks

Culture can feel fuzzy until you pin it down into actions. Here's how to turn the **Culture Blueprint** into a living, breathing system inside your company:

Step 1: Define Your Values (2–4 Max)

Don't make a laundry list. Pick the 2–4 values that actually matter in daily operations. Ask yourself:

- *What behaviors do I reward?*
- *What behaviors drive me crazy?*
- *What do I want this company to stand for when I'm not in the room?*

Write them down in plain language. Avoid clichés like "quality" or "trustworthy." Choose words your team will actually use. Make it so simple an uneducated third grader will know what you're trying to get across.

Step 2: Translate Values into Standards

Values without standards are useless. Translate each one into **observable behaviors**:

- *Integrity* → "We own mistakes immediately and fix them."
- *Ownership* → "We never bring a problem without at least one proposed solution."
- *Communication* → "Every client receives a Friday update before 5 p.m."

If you can't measure it or observe it, it's not a standard.

Step 3: Install Rituals to Reinforce Standards

Culture isn't built in a day—it's reinforced every day. Use rituals to make it stick:

- **Weekly Team Meetings:** Start with a "values in action" shout-out.
- **Quarterly Reviews:** Score every employee on both performance *and* cultural alignment.
- **Hiring Process:** Ask interview questions tied to your values. (e.g., "Tell me about a time you made a mistake and how you handled it.")
- **Recognition:** Celebrate wins that reflect values, not just project outcomes.

Rituals are the glue that make culture more than words.

Step 4: Protect the Standards

Here's the hardest part: enforcing them.

- If someone violates a cultural standard repeatedly, you must address it—even if they're a top performer.
- What you allow, you endorse. Protecting culture sometimes means letting go of toxic but talented team members.

> ⌐▶ **Real Talk:** When you define values, codify standards, and reinforce with rituals, your culture becomes self-sustaining. It stops being about what you say, and starts being about what everyone does.

That's how you move from culture by default to culture by design.

From Culture to Consistency (and the Crystal Ball)

When you design your culture with intention, everything changes.

People stop asking, *"What do I have to do?"* and start asking, *"How do we do it here?"* Your values become habits, your standards become the norm, and your rituals reinforce them until they stick. The right people stay and thrive. The wrong people end up in storage locker "b" clinging to their Swingline stapler.

At this point, you've built **The Machine.**

- Structure has replaced chaos.
- Leadership has replaced micromanagement.
- Culture has replaced drama.

But here's the secret that takes culture from *good* to *predictive.*

Most builders hire based on *résumés and gut feel.* Maybe a few reference calls. Maybe a hunch about "fit."

But what if you had a crystal ball—something that showed you, before the first interview, how someone is naturally wired to solve problems, manage details, and push projects forward?

That's what **Kolbe** gives you and why I'm a KOLBE Certified Consultant in addition to earning my ICF Certified Professional Coach Accreditation from Brown University. It's the ultimate 1-2 punch.

Kolbe isn't personality, and it isn't IQ. It measures conation—the instinctive way people take action when faced with a problem. And when you know someone's Kolbe profile, you know exactly how they'll behave under stress, how they'll communicate, and where they'll thrive—or fail—inside your structure.

I call it the crystal ball because once you see it, you can't unsee it. It's how you stop forcing people into the wrong roles and start putting them exactly where they'll succeed.

And here's the best part: once your whole team has been mapped, you'll see the friction points, the gaps, and the hidden strengths you've been missing all along.

We'll come back to this tool in depth. For now, just know this: culture is the soil. Kolbe is the lens that lets you plant the right seeds in the right place.

The $150,000 Hire That Almost Broke Him

I worked with a builder in NC who thought he'd finally solved his biggest problem: finding the right project manager.

On paper, this guy was perfect. Ten years of experience. Big jobs under his belt. Great references. He nailed the interview. The builder was so confident, he offered a generous salary package—north of $100K plus bonus—and handed over two of his most important projects immediately and breathed a sigh of relief.

But within 90 days, cracks appeared.

The new PM struggled with details, constantly missed deadlines, and clashed with the superintendents. He was great in meetings but weak in execution. Clients complained about lack of follow-through. Subs stopped trusting his scheduling - slowing down projects and turning once thrilled clients into constant complainers.

The owner doubled down—spent more of his own time "supporting" the hire, smoothing over client issues, redoing reports, even stepping back into jobsite meetings he thought he'd left behind.

By the time he let the PM go, the damage was staggering:

- **$60,000 in wasted salary**
- **$40,000 in overruns and missed change orders**
- **$50,000+ in lost profit** from projects dragged off schedule
- And hundreds of hours of stress, distraction, and sleepless nights…not to mention the future cost of missed referrals and a tarnished reputation.

One bad hire had cost him **over $150,000**—not counting the emotional toll on his family and team.

When we ran the Kolbe, it was admittedly too late when he came to me, but it was obvious: the PM's natural wiring was to brainstorm and connect—not to drive details or manage execution. He was in the wrong seat from day one.

└...➤ **Real Talk:** A Kolbe test costs less than a steak dinner (free for my clients). Using it on that one hire would have saved him six figures and months of pain.

That's why I call it the crystal ball. One bad hire can set you back a year - or worse. One Kolbe-informed hire can pay for itself—and for years of coaching—in the very first month.

Even the best culture won't carry you far without execution. Clients don't pay for good vibes—they pay for results.

That's where the next law comes in: **Law 3 – The Method.**

The Method is about **systems and execution.** It's where we take all the momentum you've built and lock it into place with processes that guarantee consistent outcomes—on time, on budget, and at your standard of excellence.

Culture creates buy-in. Kolbe gives you clarity. Systems create results.

And in the next section, we'll show you how to build the systems that turn all of this into scale.

Your Hidden Bonus Awaits

Every chapter in this book unlocks a deeper level of tools, trainings, and step-by-step guides I normally reserve for private clients. Think of it as the *hidden door* — videos, templates, and frameworks you can put to work today to implement what you're learning.

Scan the QR code if you don't like typing or visit www.builderstimemachine.com/bonus to access it now.

LAW 3

THE METHOD

You can have the right positioning. You can have a steady stream of leads. You can even be signing premium clients. But if your delivery is chaos, it all unravels.

This is where most growing builders hit the wall. They've marketed well, sold well, even landed the right jobs — but behind the scenes, it's duct tape and adrenaline. The owner is still the hub. The team is still improvising. And the client experience depends on who picked up the phone that day.

> **⌐▶ Real Talk:** Success in this business isn't about how many contracts you sign. It's about how consistently you deliver.

That's why Law 3 - **The Method** - is the discipline of turning great intentions into repeatable execution. It's the shift from being a "builder who hustles harder" to a **business that runs smoother**.

History proves it: Toyota didn't dominate by building more cars — they dominated by building a better system. Ritz-Carlton didn't lead hospitality by dazzling with chandeliers — they led by making excellence predictable.

The Method is your system. It's how you remove the scavenger hunt, kill the chaos, and replace it with confidence — for you, your team, and your clients.

The three levers inside this Law are simple but non-negotiable:

- **World-Class Client Experience** → because to the client, the experience *is* the product.

- **Predictable Job Flow** → because more jobs don't equal more profit — only efficiency does.

- **Profit & Time Mastery** → because tools and tech don't create freedom, systems and adoption do.

If positioning is The Magnet, and The Machine is the structure, then The Method is the operating system. It's the daily discipline that turns ambition into outcomes.

Without it, you scale chaos. With it, you scale clarity, confidence, and profit.

LEVER 7

WORLD-CLASS CLIENT EXPERIENCE

"People will forget what you said, people will forget what you did, but people will never forget how you made them feel."– Maya Angelou

The Scavenger Hunt Jobsite

If you've built homes for any length of time, you've seen it—or maybe you've lived it - maybe recently.

A client shows up unannounced on a Tuesday afternoon. They step onto the jobsite with excitement in their eyes, but within five minutes that excitement turns to frustration.

The trim package is sitting in the wrong room. The plumber is waiting on parts no one told the client about. There's a note scrawled on a two-by-four that only the superintendent understands. And when the client starts asking questions, the answers unravel fast:

- *"Who's showing up tomorrow?"* → "I'll check the schedule."
- *"When do we need to pick the tile?"* → "Soon… I think."
- *"Why isn't the vanity here yet?"* → "Supply chain."

Every conversation feels like a dodge. The client isn't angry about the actual delay—they're angry about being in the dark. And the worst part? Everyone on the team gives them a different answer.

That's the scavenger hunt jobsite.

The client leaves with a pit in their stomach. They start questioning the builder, the process, and whether they made a mistake choosing you in the first place. By the time they get home, they've pulled up Zillow "just to look around."

> ∟➤ **Real Talk:** Clients don't judge you by your craftsmanship. They don't crawl under the joists to admire your hangers or check the squareness of your framing. What they remember—what they talk about at dinner parties—is how the experience *felt*.

And when the experience feels like chaos? No level of craftsmanship can save you.

Most builders convince themselves their work will speak for itself. But the reality is this: **to your client, the experience *is* the product.**

Chaos Kills Trust; Systems Build It

Builders often assume that clients expect perfection. They don't. What they expect is confidence. And confidence only comes from clarity.

The real enemy of trust isn't a blown deadline or a delayed delivery—it's chaos. When a client doesn't know what's happening, they assume the worst. That uncertainty corrodes trust faster than any single mistake.

Think about it: clients can forgive weather delays. They can forgive backordered appliances. What they can't forgive is being ignored, left guessing, or discovering problems after it's too late (or thinking they did because of a broken communication cadence.)

History proves it. When **Ritz-Carlton** pioneered luxury hospitality in the early 1900s, they didn't win guests with chandeliers or marble—they won with consistency. Every guest knew their bags would be handled, their requests remembered, and their names recognized. It wasn't opulence that built trust, it was reliability.

Science confirms it too. Research published in the *Journal of Service Research* found that **reliability is the single strongest predictor of customer trust and repeat business**—more than "delight factors" or extra perks (Tax, Brown, & Chandrashekaran, 1998).

⌐▶ **Real Talk:** Chaos kills trust, systems build it.

When your business runs on systems, the client experience is no longer dependent on how available you are, or how sharp your superintendent feels that day. It's predictable. It's repeatable. And because it's predictable, clients trust it.

That's when they stop second-guessing your process and start supporting it.

Scoreboard vs. Scavenger Hunt

Imagine going to a football game where the scoreboard is broken.

The players are on the field, the refs are blowing whistles, and the fans are screaming, but nobody actually knows the score. Every few minutes, rumors fly through the stands: *"We're up by 7!"* *"No, we're down by 3!"* Chaos breaks out, confidence in the refs collapses, and pretty soon the fans stop trusting the entire game.

That's exactly how most clients feel during a custom home build. Without a scoreboard, they're forced into a scavenger hunt—digging for scraps of information from supers, admins, and the occasional rushed call from the owner. And just like those fans, their trust in the process erodes with every conflicting answer.

The solution is simple: stop running scavenger hunts. Build scoreboards.

For builders, a scoreboard has four critical pieces:

1. **One Plan** – A living schedule the client can see. Not a Gantt chart buried on your laptop, but a clear calendar of milestones, the next three weeks of activity, and the exact owner decisions due.

2. **One Source of Truth** – A central hub—portal, dashboard, or shared doc—that holds everything: drawings, selections, change orders, invoices, job photos. If it matters, it lives here.

3. **One Weekly Rhythm** – A Friday update, same format, every time. Milestones hit, what's next, owner decisions, budget/CO status, risks, and fresh photos. Not optional, not "when we get to it"—a ritual.

4. **One Issue Log** – A running list of open items, each with an owner, assignee, due date, and red/amber/green status. If it isn't on the log, it doesn't exist.

> ⌐▶ **Real Talk:** The scavenger hunt leaves clients anxious and suspicious. The scoreboard makes them fans of your process. Instead of fearing what they don't know, they relax into what they can see.

And once they trust the scoreboard, they stop looking over your shoulder. They stop micromanaging. They stop sideline-coaching. Because the score is right there in front of them, in real time.

From 12 Jobs to 19 Without Burning Out

One of my clients in MI was stuck at a ceiling. When he came to me he could handle about **12 projects at a time**—no more. Every time he added a 13th, the wheels wobbled.

His days were a blur of jobsite drive-bys. He wasn't there to check quality—he was there to keep clients calm. He would show up, answer questions, smooth over frustrations, and promise updates. The work got done, but it was chaos.

And he knew it wasn't sustainable. His family knew it too.

We implemented the **scoreboard system.**

- Every Friday by 5 p.m., clients received a written update with milestones hit, what was next, decisions needed, risks, and a link to fresh photos.

- A living 6-week look-ahead schedule was shared with every client, so they could see what was coming without calling him.

- Change orders moved into a standard process: scope in plain English, cost/time impact side by side, e-signed before work started.

- A running issue log gave everyone—clients, team, and owner—the same view of open items, who owns it, and due dates.

Within **two quarters**, the difference was dramatic.

He scaled from **12 projects to 19 concurrent jobs.** Client complaints dropped almost to zero. Subs loved the clarity and began pushing to get on his jobs because they knew the process ran smooth and ultimately made them more profitable too.

Real world: his jobsite visits went **down by nearly 60%.**

Instead of being the human fire extinguisher, he became the architect of a process that ran without him. He got his time back, his family noticed the change, and he finally had the space to think about growth instead of just surviving the week.

The work didn't get lighter. It got clearer. And clarity is what makes scale possible.

SOPs That Eliminate Chaos

> ⌐▶ **Real Talk:** World-class client experience doesn't require fancy software or a consultant's binder full of jargon. It requires **simple systems, followed religiously.**

Three SOPs are all you need to flip chaos into clarity:

1. The Weekly Client Update

This is your **keystone habit.** Every Friday by 5 p.m., clients receive an email update in the same format, every time. Not "when you remember." Not "if the super has time." Every single week, without fail.

Format:

- **Milestones Hit This Week** (3–5 bullets max)

- **What's Next** (next 7–14 days, written in plain English)
- **Decisions Needed** (list, due dates highlighted in bold)
- **Budget/Change Order Status** (current budget vs. COs, not buried in accounting language)
- **Risks/Holds** (delays, owner action items, weather, supply chain)
- **Photos** (2–3 fresh progress photos with a link to a shared folder)

Clients don't care about schedules buried in your laptop. They care about confidence. And confidence comes from predictable, consistent updates.

2. The Change Order SOP

Change orders are where profit goes to die—unless you systemize them. Most builders wing it: scribbled notes, "we'll true it up later," or handshake deals. That's how you end up eating costs, fighting with clients, and blowing timelines.

> ⌐▶ **Real Talk:** When is the last time you had a client hold the final check because they were surprised by the final bill... which turned into a fight... which kept you up at night... which ate away at time you could have been putting new deals together and networking or working "on" the business - it very likely started at the beginning of the job.

Three Steps to Bulletproof COs:

1. **Scope in Plain English** – Write it so the client could explain it back to you. "Add one recessed can in master bath above vanity" beats "Lighting adjustment."

2. **Cost + Time Impact Side by Side** – Show the price *and* the delay (if any). Clients make better decisions when they see the trade-off clearly and having this ever growing list is pure gold at the end of a project when they're pointing the finger at you for being "behind".

3. **E-Sign + Deposit Before Work Begins** – No signature, no work. No deposit, no materials ordered.

This isn't bureaucracy. It's protection—for you *and* your client.

3. The Issue Log

The issue log is your **company's memory.** Instead of chasing sticky notes, texts, and verbal promises, you have one place where every open item lives.

Columns:

- Issue description
- Owner (client, builder, sub)
- Assignee (who's responsible)
- Due date
- Status (Red/Amber/Green)

Process:

- Review internally at your weekly team meeting.
- Highlight only the top issues in the Friday client update.
- If it's not on the log, it doesn't exist.

The issue log prevents forgotten promises, eliminates finger-pointing, and gives you a paper trail when accountability matters most.

Together, these three SOPs are the difference between chaos and confidence. They aren't complicated. They aren't expensive. But they demand discipline.

And that discipline is what creates a **world-class client experience**.

With Clients Confident, Now You Can Streamline Flow

Once your clients can see the score, everything changes.

They stop calling you for updates because they already know what's happening. They stop micromanaging your supers because they trust the process. They stop peppering you with "what's next?" questions because the answer is already in their inbox every Friday at 5 p.m and in turn they stop calling you Sunday at 3pm while you're at your kids t-ball game.

In short, the chaos evaporates.

And when chaos evaporates, so does the pressure that kept you capped. Instead of spending hours every week putting out fires and calming nerves, you suddenly have free bandwidth to focus on what actually matters: **moving work through the system.**

This is where the real scaling lever shows up. Because client communication is the front-end system, but job flow is the back-end engine.

> ⌐▶ **Real Talk:** The builders trap…the moment clients feel calm… they immediately take on more jobs. But if the flow behind the scenes is still broken, all they've done is turn their chaos into *bigger* chaos.

The next lever is about avoiding that trap. It's about learning that **more jobs don't equal more profit.** And until you master job flow, growth just breaks you faster.

That's why the next chapter focuses on **Predictable Job Flow.**

We'll look at why scaling without flow is the fastest way to burn cash, how to identify the projects that actually make you money, and how to design a business model that delivers profit and freedom—not just volume.

Because once your clients are confident, the only thing left to streamline is the engine that delivers the work.

And that's exactly where we're headed next.

Your Hidden Bonus Awaits

Every chapter in this book unlocks a deeper level of tools, trainings, and step-by-step guides I normally reserve for private clients. Think of it as the *hidden door* — videos, templates, and frameworks you can put to work today to implement what you're learning.

Scan the QR code if you don't like typing or visit www.builderstimemachine.com/bonus to access it now.

LEVER 8

PREDICTABLE JOB FLOW: SCALING CHAOS $\longrightarrow$ BROKE FASTER.

"More isn't better. Better is better." – Simon Sinek

Scaling Chaos   Broke Faster

Ask any builder what they'd do with more jobs, and most will grin and say, *"I'd be rich."* The assumption is simple: more jobs mean more revenue, and more revenue means more profit.

> ⌐▶ **Real Talk:** Here's what really happens when you scale chaos: you don't get rich—you get broke faster.

I've seen it play out a hundred times. A builder finally breaks through a ceiling—lands three more jobs, doubles their backlog, stacks their calendar. For a few weeks, it feels like momentum. The phones are buzzing, deposits are coming in, the team is scrambling. It looks like growth.

Then the cracks start showing. Estimates drag out. Subs get stretched thin. Clients don't get updates, so they start calling every day. Change orders pile up without signatures. Jobs stall waiting on selections. The very systems that were "good enough" at five or six projects collapse under the weight of twelve.

And the worst part? The builder is working harder than ever, but the bank account isn't moving. In fact, it's draining. Because when you multiply broken systems, you multiply waste.

I sat across from a client once who told me through clenched teeth, *"Rod, I thought doubling my jobs would double my profits. Instead, it doubled my stress and cut my margin in half."*

That's the painful reality: growth exposes weakness. If the flow of jobs isn't predictable, more work doesn't create freedom—it creates the exact opposite.

It's the illusion of progress masking the reality of chaos.

And until builders internalize that truth, they'll keep running faster on a treadmill that isn't moving forward.

More Jobs ≠ More Profit

In construction, we're conditioned to chase volume. More contracts signed, more jobs started, more dirt moving—that's how most builders measure success. It feels like progress, but it's often just motion.

> └┈▶ **Real Talk:** More jobs don't equal more profit.

History proves it. In the 1980s, **General Motors** was the largest carmaker in the world. Their strategy was simple: build more models, open more plants, flood the market. For a while, the numbers looked good—until the cracks showed. Quality dipped, inefficiency ballooned, and Toyota, with fewer models but laser-focused systems, overtook them in profit per vehicle. GM had volume, Toyota had flow. Guess who won?

PS: If you wonder why I have so many car company examples... it's because I have a car problem... specifically a classic car problem... but I digress.

Science reinforces it.

A Harvard Business Review analysis of growth companies found that **firms with unbalanced scaling—adding volume without tightening operations—suffered profit erosion at more than twice the rate of disciplined peers** (HBR, "Why Companies That Grow Fast Fail Faster," 2012).

Translation: if you grow without flow, the weight of inefficiency crushes you.

Builders live this every day. The reflex is to say yes to every lead, pile jobs into the calendar, and hope profit shows up at the end. But what shows up instead? Frantic weeks, angry clients, exhausted crews, and margin that bleeds away one missed detail at a time.

> ⌐▸ **Real Talk:** Volume doesn't create profit—clarity does.

Profit comes from sequencing the right jobs, at the right margins, in a flow your systems can handle. Without that, more jobs just accelerate your losses.

When you really absorb this belief shift, everything changes. You stop bragging about how many jobs you're juggling and start caring about how much margin each job is delivering. You stop chasing "busy" and start engineering "profitable."

That's when you start to build a business instead of just building houses.

Budget Mastery and Efficiency: The Hidden Engines of Profit

In construction, one of the most dangerous assumptions is that more jobs equal more profit. Builders fall into the trap of thinking the answer to margin pressure is volume—if five jobs make a little money, surely ten jobs will make twice as much. But what actually happens is the opposite: more jobs often magnify waste, multiply inefficiency, and shrink profit.

> ⌐⋯► **Real Talk:** Profit doesn't come from job count, it comes from job flow. And two levers drive that flow more than any others—budget mastery and operational efficiency.

Budget Mastery: The GPS of Profitability

Too many builders treat the budget like a static document created at the start of the job. They price the project, shake hands with the client, file the estimate, and hope the numbers hold. But in construction, hope is not a strategy.

Budgets should be living, breathing roadmaps—your GPS for profitability. Just as no driver would embark on a cross-country trip without recalibrating for traffic jams, weather delays, or detours, no builder should run a project without revisiting budgets regularly.

When you don't, small variances snowball into major problems. A missed allowance here, a delayed decision there—before long, your margins are gone. Worse, repeated overruns lead estimators to pad future bids, driving prices up and win rates down. Clients grow frustrated. Referrals dry up. The ripple effect of poor budget management haunts a business for years.

The solution is simple, but rarely practiced: standardized budget reviews. Weekly for active jobs. Monthly for longer projects. These reviews should track not just dollars, but timing. A cost incurred too early can wreck cash flow just as badly as an outright overrun.

Modern software makes this process nearly effortless. Real-time tracking, mobile logging from the field, and automatic variance alerts turn budgeting into a daily discipline rather than a yearly panic. The most profitable builders aren't the ones with the biggest pipelines— they're the ones who treat budgets as living systems.

Efficiency: The Hidden Profit Center

If budgets are your GPS, efficiency is the engine that drives the vehicle taking us there. And here's the sobering reality: most construction crews spend less than 40% of their time on direct, value-adding work. The other 60% is wasted on searching for materials, waiting on instructions, and redoing mistakes that should have been caught the first time.

That wasted time is more expensive than the dumpsters full of scrap lumber and drywall. It's the silent killer of margin.

The first step in fixing it is to measure it. Builders are often shocked when they track where hours really go. Highly skilled carpenters burn hours hunting for tools. Subs are waiting half a day because the prior trade wasn't finished. Supers fielding endless calls for answers buried in disorganized paperwork. You spending 20 hours a week driving all over town for "urgent" meetings. Once you see it, you can't unsee it.

Then the solutions reveal themselves. Daily huddles to clarify tasks. Organized staging areas to eliminate scavenger hunts for materials. Clear schedules with accountability for each trade. Even small changes, such as requiring field photos in weekly updates, can reclaim hours that would otherwise be lost.

Think of your site as a production line. In manufacturing, every step is analyzed, every handoff scrutinized. A misaligned part on one station isn't tolerated because it slows the entire assembly. Yet on job sites, we tolerate sloppiness that ripples through every trade behind it. When you shift to a production mindset, efficiency becomes a profit multiplier instead of a margin leak.

Why More Jobs Break You Faster

When a builder scales without mastering budget and efficiency, the cracks widen into chasms. Every inefficiency gets multiplied. Every hidden cost spreads across more jobs. What felt like growth quickly turns into burnout, client frustration, and shrinking profit.

Builders who don't understand this mistake activity for achievement. They brag about running 15 jobs but whisper about their bank balance.

> ⌐▶ **Real Talk:** Volume without flow is a treadmill. You run faster, but you're not going anywhere.

By contrast, builders who master budget discipline and efficiency flip the equation. They make more money with fewer jobs, not fewer dollars with more. They build reputations for quality and reliability, which generates more of the only marketing that matters: a solid reputation. And they create businesses that don't collapse under the weight of their own ambition.

> ⌐⋯▶ **Real Talk:** Profit doesn't come from doing more work— it comes from doing work better.

When you treat your budgets like living maps, inefficiency like a disease to be measured and eliminated, and job flow like the true measure of success, you stop confusing busyness with business. You stop planting new seeds without tending the ones already in the ground.

That's when the treadmill stops. That's when profit compounds. And that's when you finally stop being owned by your jobs and start owning your business.

If you did the exact same number of jobs this year as you did last, at the same top line revenue, but you put 5% more of that directly in your bank account - how would that change your circumstances? Your family? Your impact? Your legacy?

Dropping Low-Margin Jobs = +22% Profit

I worked with a builder who was running what looked like a thriving company: trucks on the road, job signs all over town, his phone ringing off the hook. From the outside, he looked like the poster child for growth. But when we pulled the numbers apart, the truth came out—he was working harder than ever and taking home less than he had three years earlier.

The culprit? Low-margin jobs clogging his pipeline.

Like so many owners, he'd fallen into the trap of saying yes to almost every opportunity that came across his desk. Kitchen remodel for a past client? Yes. Deck replacement down the road? Yes. A low-bid spec build just to keep the crews busy? Yes.

Each job covered some overhead and felt like momentum. But when we ran the actual job costing, the reality was brutal: half of his projects were barely breaking even, and some were actively losing money.

Together we drew a line in the sand. From that day forward, his company would only take projects that met three criteria:

1. The margins were healthy.
2. The work aligned with his team's strengths and the 12 month goals for the business.
3. The client fit his ideal profile.

It was uncomfortable at first. Saying no always is. He worried about turning away "easy revenue". But within a few months, the numbers spoke for themselves. By trimming low-margin jobs, he freed up his team's capacity for higher-value projects. Overhead stopped being spread thin across a dozen distractions and was instead focused on profitable work.

The result? A 22% increase in net profit within the first year—without adding a single new client, estimator, or superintendent. Same number of jobs? No. Fewer jobs, actually. But better ones.

That's the paradox most builders miss: fewer projects at higher margins create more profit than chasing every job that comes along.

This client didn't just make more money—he bought back his sanity. His staff wasn't drowning in tiny change orders. His best subs weren't tied up on low-value jobs as "favors" to past clients. And his evenings stopped being consumed by putting out fires on projects that never should have been signed in the first place.

It's proof that when you shift your focus from volume to flow, profit follows.

Job Costing, Profit Gap Calculation, and the Genius Model Revisited

Dropping low-margin jobs frees capacity and increases profit. But how do you know which jobs to keep and which ones to cut? This is where tactical tools—job costing, profit gap calculations, and the Genius Model we already covered—come into play.

1. Job Costing: The X-Ray for Your Business

Most builders run their company on what I call *bank-balance accounting*: if there's money in the account, things must be fine. The problem is, you can "look fine" while bleeding margin on every job.

True job costing means tracking every dollar of revenue, labor, materials, and overhead against each project—not just once at the end, but in real time. When you do this, you uncover hidden truths:

- That "easy deck job" your team knocked out in three weeks? It barely covered overhead.
- The remodel that "felt good" because the client was happy? It paid $6 an hour once all labor was counted.
- The custom home that looked like a win at $1.8M? It lost $30K in slippage because allowances and change orders weren't tracked - and there was a battle over the final bill.

Job costing is the X-ray that reveals which projects are strengthening your business and which ones are quietly breaking it.

2. Profit Gap Calculation: Quantifying the Waste

Once you've got real job costing data, the next step is calculating your *profit gap*: the difference between what you *should* be making based on your pricing and overhead, and what you're actually making once waste, inefficiency, and low-margin jobs are factored in.

For one client, the gap was $480,000 in a single year. Almost half a million dollars that *should* have been profit, but leaked away through underbidding, change order slippage, and jobs that never should've been signed.

When you can put a number on your profit gap, it becomes impossible to ignore. That number is the cost of not running your business on flow.

3. The Genius Model: Profitable, Enjoyable, Desired

Finally, the Genius Model we discussed earlier is what gives you a front line filter for deciding which jobs to pursue. Every project should be run through three questions:

- **Profitable:** Does this job meet or exceed my target margins?
- **Enjoyable:** Does my team like doing this type of work, or will it drain morale?
- **Desired:** Is this the kind of project that positions us where we want to be in the market?

Jobs that score "yes" across the board go to the top of the list. Jobs that score "no" on two or three? Those are distractions disguised as revenue.

When builders adopt the Genius Model, something remarkable happens. They stop chasing every shiny object. They stop saying yes out of fear and start saying no out of strategy. The result is fewer, better jobs—and more money in the bank.

The Tactical Takeaway: Don't let volume fool you. Track your true job costs. Calculate your profit gap. Run every opportunity through the Genius Model. Do that consistently, and you'll discover what my most successful clients already know: **profit isn't about how many jobs you do—it's about doing the right jobs, the right way.**

From Chaos to Control

Imagine your business a year from now. You're no longer juggling twenty jobs just to keep the lights on. Instead, you're running a tighter slate of projects—each one profitable, each one aligned with your strengths, each one positioning you exactly where you want to be in the market.

Your team isn't buried under a mountain of busywork, scrambling to keep up. They're focused, efficient, and confident because the jobs they're working on have structure, clarity, and margin built in. Subs respect your schedules. Clients actually enjoy the process. And instead of walking job sites with your stomach in knots, you're walking them with a sense of control.

This is what happens when job flow becomes predictable. You stop reacting to problems and start engineering outcomes. You know your numbers. You know which projects to pursue and which ones to decline. You've cut the dead weight and created a business that compounds profit instead of bleeding it.

> ⌐▶ **Real Talk:** When flow is optimized, you finally get to focus on the highest-value lever of all—profit and time mastery.

That's the transition from being a builder to becoming a CEO. Not someone who survives job to job, but someone who shapes a business designed to last.

Your Hidden Bonus Awaits

Every chapter in this book unlocks a deeper level of tools, trainings, and step-by-step guides I normally reserve for private clients. Think of it as the *hidden door* — videos, templates, and frameworks you can put to work today to implement what you're learning.

Scan the QR code if you don't like typing or visit www.builderstimemachine.com/bonus to access it now.

LEVER 9
PROFIT & TIME MASTERY

"Technology is only as good as the culture that adopts it."
- Rodric Lenhart

The Software Graveyard

Walk into almost any builder's office and you'll find the same thing: a digital graveyard of software subscriptions.

Buildertrend. CoConstruct. JobTread. Procore. Monday. Asana. Trello. The list goes on. Each program was bought with the promise of "this will fix it." Each one rolled out with enthusiasm, a few weeks of use, then quietly abandoned.

One client of mine had spent well over six figures on software tools in three years—and not one of them was being used consistently by his team. They sat like rusting tools in the shed, still sharp but collecting dust. Why? Because the programs weren't the real problem.

Builders buy software thinking it will solve inefficiency. But what actually happens is the inefficiency just shifts platforms. Instead of

131

disorganized spreadsheets, you get disorganized dashboards. Instead of missed texts, you get missed notifications. The chaos doesn't go away—it just moves to a new app.

And the cost isn't just the subscription fee. It's the hours wasted onboarding a team that never buys in. It's the frustration of trying to manage multiple platforms that don't talk to each other. It's the stress of realizing you've spent thousands of dollars and hundreds of hours chasing tools that never delivered.

That graveyard is more than wasted money—it's a mirror. It reflects the truth that tools don't create profit. Systems do.

Tech Is Only Valuable If the Team Uses It

The biggest myth in construction technology is that buying software equals solving problems. It doesn't.

Too many builders believe that the right platform will finally bring order to their chaos. But technology is only as valuable as the team's ability—and willingness—to use it. If adoption is low, the software isn't an asset; it's just another expense.

I've seen it time and again. An owner gets excited about a shiny new program. They sign the contract, sit through the onboarding calls, and feel the dopamine rush of "finally, a solution."

But then reality hits. The supers won't log in from the field. The admin doesn't trust the system, so she keeps her own spreadsheet on the side. The project managers find it clunky and revert to group texts and emails. Within months, the software is abandoned, but the credit card charge keeps running.

> ⌐┅▶ **Real Talk:** The shift is recognizing that the tool is never the solution by itself. It's the people behind the tool that make it work. A hammer doesn't build a house—carpenters do. And if your team isn't bought in, trained, and supported, no piece of software will save you.

Profit and time mastery come not from stacking tech subscriptions, but from creating adoption. From building habits. From making the system so simple, so embedded in daily life, that not using it would feel impossible.

Until you make that shift, your software graveyard will keep growing. Once you do, every dollar invested in tools turns into hours saved, mistakes prevented, and profit captured.

Tech Stack Adoption With Field Buy-In

If technology by itself isn't the solution, what is? The framework is simple: **adopt your tech stack with field buy-in, not just office enthusiasm.**

Here's how it works:

1. Start With the Field, Not the Office

Most builders make the mistake of choosing software based on what looks good in the office. But the truth is, if the field won't use it, the system dies before it starts. Adoption must begin with the people swinging hammers, walking sites, and making daily decisions. If they find it useful, it spreads. If they resist, it fails.

2. Solve One Problem at a Time

Don't dump an entire suite of features on your team. Instead, start small. Pick the single biggest pain point—maybe it's daily logs, change orders, or schedule updates—and make the new system solve *that one thing* better than whatever came before. Once the team sees success, you can layer in the next feature.

3. Train Until It's Second Nature

Software training isn't a one-hour webinar at kickoff. It's a process. Ride-along coaching with supers. Step-by-step guides for admins. Weekly check-ins to reinforce the habit until it sticks. Training isn't about information—it's about repetition until the new behavior feels easier than the old one.

4. Appoint Champions, Not Police

Instead of making tech adoption about compliance ("use this or else"), appoint champions in your team who naturally embrace the system. Let them model the behavior, share wins, and encourage peers. People follow people more than policies.

5. Audit and Adjust

Finally, adoption isn't set-and-forget. Audit usage. Ask the team where friction still exists. Adjust workflows to make it easier. The goal isn't perfection—it's consistency.

When you follow this framework, your software doesn't sit idle in the graveyard. It becomes an actual force multiplier. Buildertrend stops being a dashboard you ignore and becomes the heartbeat of your business. JobTread stops being a cost and starts being a command center.

> ⌐➤ **Real Talk:** The difference isn't in the code. It's in the culture.

Buildertrend Rollout   60% Fewer Owner Site Visits

One of my clients, a custom builder running about a dozen million-plus jobs at once, was on the brink of burnout. He was personally visiting nearly every job site multiple times a week just to keep things moving. His truck had become his second office, and his evenings were consumed by catching up on updates that should've been handled during the day.

When we looked closer, the issue wasn't that his team was incapable—it was that they were blind. Everyone had a different version of "the truth." Subs relied on text threads. The superintendent scribbled notes in a spiral notebook. The office admin updated spreadsheets that nobody in the field ever saw. And every time something slipped through the cracks, the owner had to show up in person to get things back on track.

We decided to roll out Buildertrend (insert any capable program here by the way). But we didn't just buy licenses and hope. We followed the framework:

- We started small, focusing only on daily logs and photo updates.
- We trained the supers until posting photos became as natural as grabbing their tape measure.
- We appointed one of the younger project managers—already tech-comfortable—as the adoption champion.
- We held short weekly huddles to review wins and refine the process.

Within 90 days, the transformation was dramatic. Every active job had daily photo updates in the system. Clients could log in and see progress without calling the owner or PM. Subs knew where they stood because schedules were updated in real time. The office stopped chasing information, and the owner finally stopped making constant site visits "just to check."

The result? A 60% reduction in owner site visits. More importantly, the owner reclaimed dozens of hours each month—time he could reinvest in higher-level strategy instead of firefighting in the field.

The lesson wasn't that Buildertrend was magic software. The lesson was that adoption, done right, created leverage. The tech became the system, and the system created freedom.

Audit Stack, Phased Rollout, Training Plan

Software isn't the problem—and it's not the solution either. The key is how you implement it. Builders who master profit and time don't chase shiny new platforms; they build adoption plans as carefully as they build houses.

Here's how to do it:

1. Audit Your Current Tech Stack

Start by listing every piece of software you're paying for—whether you think you're "using it" or not. Include project management, accounting, estimating, CRM, even apps your team has downloaded on their own. For each tool, ask three questions:

- Is it being used consistently by at least 80% of the team?
- Does it directly reduce time, errors, or overhead?
- Is it integrated with the other systems we rely on?

Anything that fails those tests is either eliminated or earmarked for a relaunch with a new adoption plan.

2. Choose One Anchor Platform

You don't need five different tools doing the same thing. You need one anchor platform that becomes the central hub of your business—your "command center." For most builders, this is Buildertrend, CoConstruct, JobTread or Procore. The anchor is where schedules live, where communication happens, and where truth is tracked.

3. Roll Out in Phases, Not All at Once

Think of adoption like framing a house: you don't install the roof before the walls are up. Start with one or two core features—daily logs, change orders, schedules—and nail those down. Once the team is fluent, layer in the next feature. Phased rollout prevents overwhelm and builds confidence.

4. Train, Train, Train

Most builders fail here. They run one kickoff webinar and assume the team is ready. Wrong. Real training is ongoing:

- **Ride-alongs** with supers to show how to log updates in the field.
- **Checklists** for admins to follow every week.
- **Short weekly huddles** to reinforce and refine.
- Training isn't about information; it's about creating muscle memory.

5. Build Champions, Not Enforcers

Adoption spreads through influence, not mandates. Find the person on your team who naturally embraces tech and make them the champion. Let them model the behavior, share wins, and encourage peers. When the team sees that adoption makes *their* lives easier—not just the owner's—they'll follow.

6. Review and Refine

Finally, build a feedback loop. Every quarter, review what's working, where friction exists, and what needs to improve. Adoption isn't a one-time event; it's a living system that evolves as your company scales.

When you follow this tactical plan, software stops being another graveyard expense and becomes a living operating system. Your team spends less time chasing information, clients trust you more, and you as the owner buy back hours every week. That's how you turn technology into profit and time mastery.

Your Hidden Bonus Awaits

Every chapter in this book unlocks a deeper level of tools, trainings, and step-by-step guides I normally reserve for private clients. Think of it as the *hidden door* — videos, templates, and frameworks you can put to work today to implement what you're learning.

Scan the QR code if you don't like typing or visit www.builderstimemachine.com/bonus to access it now.

FROM BUILDER TO CEO

You do not rise to the level of your goals. You fall to the level of your systems." — James Clear

Picture your weeks six months from now. You're no longer buried under endless site visits, late-night texts, or software bills that feel like wasted money. Instead, your business runs on a clear, integrated system that your team actually uses.

Jobs are tracked in real time. Clients log in and get answers without calling you. Subs show up when they're supposed to because schedules are visible and enforced. And your team? They're not chasing paper, texts, or ten different apps. They're working inside one command center where truth lives.

The result is freedom. Fewer mistakes. Fewer fires. Fewer wasted hours.

But more importantly—**you've made the leap from builder to CEO.**

Because CEOs don't get paid for site visits. CEOs don't get paid for retyping notes into a dozen places. CEOs get paid for thinking, leading, and making decisions that multiply value. And with profit and time mastered, you now have the breathing room to do exactly that.

This is the point where your company stops depending on your hustle and starts compounding through systems. It's where the ceiling breaks. It's where you stop being trapped in a job you own and start owning a business that works for you.

With The Magnet dialed in, The Machine structured, and The Method systemized, you've done what most builders never achieve. You've created scale with sanity. Profit with freedom. Growth without chaos.

This is the escape plan—your shift from overwhelmed operator to strategic CEO. And the best part? You did it without burning yourself out or sacrificing the life you were building for in the first place.

From Blueprint to Building Your Legacy

We've made it to the end of our journey together—and what a journey it's been. When I first set out to write this book, I knew the path from overwhelmed operator to strategic CEO wasn't just about techniques or frameworks. It was about reshaping how you see yourself, your business, and your role in both.

> ⌐··▶ **Real Talk:** The hardest transitions are never about software, spreadsheets, or systems. They're about you. The toughest job site you'll ever manage is the six inches between your ears. That's where the real work of scaling happens.

Throughout these pages, we've walked together through the 3 Laws and 9 Levers—the framework designed to turn your construction company from an expensive prison into a wealth-generating asset that actually serves your life.

But before you close this book and move on, let's pause to remember what really matters:

- **Leadership precedes systems.** Without your evolution as a leader, no process in the world can save you from operational quicksand. You must grow before your business can. Period. Full stop.

- **Focus trumps diversification.** Those who plant their lighthouse in the market—who become known for one thing—create a magnetic pull that makes selling nearly obsolete. The riches really are in the niches.

- **Strategy must replace firefighting.** The moment you stop reacting to today's chaos and start architecting tomorrow's moves, you create advantages your competitors can't catch up to.

Together, these laws form the architectural blueprint for a business that scales with profit, freedom, and sanity. But here's the thing: **blueprints without action are just paper dreams.**

This is the moment where you decide if this book was just an interesting read—or if it's the starting point of your escape plan. Many builders get stuck right here. They nod, they agree, they highlight passages… and then they go back to doing things the old way.

But if you've read this far, I know you're not interested in staying stuck. You're not one of the few who do versus the many who talk. You want the business—and the life—you set out to build when you first picked up a hammer. And that's why my challenge to you is simple: **don't try to do this alone.**

I've spent decades walking builders through these exact transitions, helping them implement the 3 Laws and 9 Levers inside their companies. If you're serious about turning these blueprints into your reality, now is the time to reach out.

Because legacies aren't built on paper. They're built in action.

Turning Knowledge Into Action

Now comes the part that separates dreamers from 8 and 9 figure builders: **execution.**

I've seen it too many times. A construction entrepreneur attends a conference, or finishes a book like this one, filled with insights, fired up with new ideas—and then Monday morning hits. The phone rings, the subs are late, the inspector red-tags a job, and all that inspiration gets buried under the grind.

Knowledge without application is nothing more than wasted potential. The difference between the builders who break through and those who stay stuck isn't intelligence, talent, or even resources.

It's action.

Start small, but start now. Pick just **one lever** that resonated most deeply with you, and commit to it for the next 30 days. Maybe it's clarifying your niche so your market finally knows what you stand for. Maybe it's building your first scoreboard so your team can see what winning looks like. Whatever it is, put blinders on and implement it fully before you move to the next.

Remember my client from CO? When he and I first started working together, he was doing about $3.2 million a year—on paper, successful. But behind the scenes, he was drowning in 70+ hour work weeks, and his family barely saw him. We started with just one thing: The Magnet. He didn't touch anything else until it was humming.

Six months later, his pipeline was stronger than ever, filled with higher-quality clients, and his personal involvement in sales had dropped by 60%. Over the next two years, he stacked the other levers one by one. The result? He grew past $11 million in revenue while cutting his workload to under 35 hours a week. That's not theory—that's execution.

> ⌐▶ **Real Talk:** This transformation isn't easy. If it were, every builder in your market would already be doing it. You'll face resistance—internally and externally. Your team will push back against change. Some clients will question your new systems. And in your own head, that voice of doubt will whisper: "Maybe it's easier just to keep doing things the old way."

But resistance is the price of growth. It's the friction that shapes you into the kind of leader your future business requires.

I know this firsthand. When I sold my first company, I felt both freedom and fear. The systems and team I'd built were running without me—which was the goal—but I couldn't help wondering: did that mean I wasn't needed anymore? Builders wrestle with that same fear when they step back from being the firefighter and start leading like a CEO.

> ⌐▶ **Real Talk:** Becoming strategically unnecessary doesn't diminish your value—it multiplies it. It frees you to focus on vision, growth, and opportunity. It gives you back the most precious resource you'll ever own - your time.

And that's why I'll challenge you again: don't try to white-knuckle this transition alone. The fastest, surest way to implement these levers is to work with someone who's guided dozens of builders through the same journey. I've helped men and women just like you go from chaos and 70-hour weeks to multi-million-dollar businesses they actually enjoy running.

If you're serious about turning this knowledge into action scan the QR code below and let's hop on a 20 Minute Blueprint call. It's where every builder you read about in these pages started. Nothing to buy. Just clarity and a real plan. Let's build your legacy together—one lever at a time.

Beyond the Bottom Line

We've spent this entire book digging into strategies, systems, and structures—everything it takes to escape the chaos and step fully into your role as CEO. But before we close, I want to remind you of something even more important: the **purpose behind it all.**

In my work with builders across the country, I've noticed a clear pattern. The ones who successfully make the leap from operator to CEO don't do it just for profit. They do it for *purpose.*

They scale their businesses not just to pad the bottom line and buy a new truck but to create more freedom, more impact, and more meaning.

I've coached builders who used their new time freedom to actually be present with their kids before they left for college. Others launched nonprofits, scholarships, or community initiatives that left a mark far beyond their job sites. Some took younger builders under their wing, mentoring the next generation of entrepreneurs. And a few, like me, found their highest purpose in helping fellow builders break free from the same operational traps that once kept them chained.

Your "why" may look different. Maybe it's about building generational wealth. Maybe it's about coaching your kid's baseball team. Maybe it's about proving to yourself—and to everyone watching—that you can scale without selling your soul. That you're an owner - not an operator.

Whatever your deeper why is, keep it front and center. Because on the hard days—and there will be hard days—it won't be systems or dashboards that pull you through. It'll be your vision of the life you're building beyond the business.

I'll never forget standing on the beach in Thailand flip-flops in the sand, watching the sunset after closing a major deal that changed my company's trajectory. The business milestone was satisfying. But what made that moment unforgettable was knowing the ripple effect—how my success would create opportunities for my team, my family, and my community. That's the real scoreboard.

And that's why this book can't end here. Because if you've made it this far, you don't just want a profitable business—you want a meaningful one.

So the next step is yours: decide if you'll keep this knowledge on the shelf, or if you'll put it to work building not just profit, but a legacy.

If you're ready, I'd be honored to walk alongside you and help you implement the 3 Laws and 9 Levers inside your business.

Because at the end of the day, the bottom line isn't the real finish line. **The real win is the life you create—and the legacy you leave—beyond the business.**

Your Next Steps

As we conclude our time together, I want to leave you with three specific actions to take within the next week:

1. **Schedule a full day away from your business** to reflect on which of the 3 Laws most challenges your current approach, and which of the 9 Levers would create the greatest immediate impact if implemented. Phone off. No distractions. If you think that's impossible - it's the surest sign that you need it more than you admit.

2. **Identify your first "Minimal Viable System"** to implement. Remember, perfectionism is the enemy of progress. Start small, iterate quickly, and improve continuously.

3. **Find accountability**. Whether it's joining our Builder's Boardroom, finding another mentor, or simply partnering with another builder who's on the same journey, transformation rarely happens in isolation.

The construction industry has given me some of my greatest challenges and most rewarding victories. The frameworks in this book aren't theoretical concepts created in a classroom—they're battle-tested strategies forged in the trenches alongside builders just like you.

You have everything you need to make this transition. The blueprints are drawn. The materials are gathered. The foundation is set. Now it's time to build.

Your future self—the strategic CEO who leads with clarity, purpose, and freedom—is waiting. Don't keep him waiting too long.

Remember…

"The best time to plant a tree was 20 years ago. The second best time is now." — Chinese Proverb

Your Hidden Bonus Awaits

Every chapter in this book unlocks a deeper level of tools, trainings, and step-by-step guides I normally reserve for private clients. Think of it as the *hidden door* — videos, templates, and frameworks you can put to work today to implement what you're learning.

Scan the QR code if you don't like typing or visit www.builderstimemachine.com/bonus to access it now.

ABOUT THE AUTHOR

Rodric Lenhart is a serial entrepreneur, best selling author, international speaker, philanthropist, and trusted advisor to high-performing business owners who refuse to settle for the ordinary. His journey—from a small-town upbringing, to building and selling multiple companies, to launching a global foundation and multiple bestselling books - reflects a central theme: success is not just about money, but about freedom, clarity, and living life on your own terms.

Rodric grew up in Michigan, raised by a mother whose adventurous spirit and love of travel would later inspire his life's philanthropic mission and the creation of Send A Student Leader Abroad (to which 100% of the profits from this book and Million Dollar Flip Flops are donated). As a teenager, he joined a student trip abroad—a life-changing journey that opened his eyes to the power of perspective, culture, and possibility. That spark would fuel his drive for freedom, both in business and in life and later take him to some 65 countries.

Entrepreneurship was never just a career choice; it was in his DNA. Rodric started hustling early, built multiple businesses, and learned the hard truths of success—both the victories and the sacrifices.

Today, his mission is to help others avoid the traps he once fell into and accelerate their own path to freedom.

Through his coaching programs, international speaking tours, and his foundation *Send a Student Leader Abroad*, Rodric empowers business leaders to scale their companies without sacrificing their lives. His work centers on one core belief: **true wealth is measured not by what you earn, but by the life you design.**

DISCLAIMER

The case studies, stories, and examples in this book are all based on real experiences of clients and builders I've worked with. Their results are theirs, not promises of yours. Every business is different, and success depends on many variables: effort, market conditions, timing, decision-making, and sometimes just plain luck.

Nothing in these pages should be taken as a guarantee of specific outcomes. While some builders scaled from $3M to $11M (and beyond), others chose different paths, hit unexpected obstacles, or grew at a slower pace. That's life in business.

This book is for educational and informational purposes only. It does not constitute legal, financial, or professional advice. Always consult with qualified professionals before making big decisions.

And finally—because lawyers want me to say this—results aren't typical. But then again, neither are the builders who actually do the work.

www.ingramcontent.com/pod-product-compliance
Lightning Source LLC
Chambersburg PA
CBHW071556200326
41519CB00021BB/6770